A Taste of Generation Yum

How the Millennial Generation's Love for Organic Fare, Celebrity Chefs and Microbrews Will Make or Break the Future of Food

by

Eve Turow

"Absolutely the engine of dining, even fine dining now, across the board, is this generation of seemingly food obsessed people who are willing to drive an hour and a half for a sweet taco or save up money—that my generation would have spent on cocaine—to go to Le Bernardin."

—Anthony Bourdain

Introduction
Get a Real Taste of Generation Yum

I always knew not to worry if my pants didn't button in January. Soon enough I'd return to school and my waist would reliably shrink to its proper circumference. Winter break was a time to indulge in the things my mother kept stocked: fresh deli bagels and Jewish-certified cream cheese, chocolate cake, chips and, of course, her encouragement to eat. Back at Amherst College, food simply wasn't important. Afternoons, I'd head to the dining hall, avoid the rumored grade D meat and pile gelatinous brown rice, pre-cooked mushy pinto beans, blocks of bouncy tofu and unlabeled white shredded cheese into a red ceramic bowl. After dousing with salt, I'd place it in the microwave, sometimes alongside a bowl of raw broccoli, and zap my way to an edible meal.

A recent trip back to Amherst revealed an entirely new perspective on the place I had called home for four years. I noticed the nearby farms, bountiful weekend farmer's market, the greenhouse tacked to the back of the science library. Turns out, during the years of my life spent most reliably surrounded by fresh produce, I instead was eating pulpous mush. And I had been ok with that.

Now, I look back in disgust. If College Eve were Today Eve, I would have pulled a recipe for that bowl of rice from Pinterest or Epicurious. I would have tweeted a picture of it using Instagram filters and maybe written a Facebook post asking for more innovative salad bar ideas. I would have added some experimental hot sauce that I assume college students now whip up in dorm rooms. And I definitely would have visited the nearby farms to learn about the harvest and gather its bounty. The reason for this is simple: After college, food transitioned from a means of subsistence to a defining characteristic of my being. Food became me. In fact, food became the crux of my generation.

A quick Google search of the word "Millennials" returns a string of results reflecting curiosity, discontent and even disgust with America's newest adult generation: polls like "How Millennial Are You?" and articles titled, "Why Can't Millennials Find Jobs?" A *TIME* magazine cover story was called, "The me, me, me generation: Millennials are lazy, entitled narcissists who still live with their parents; Why they'll save us all." There is a published book with the title *The Dumbest Generation: How the Digital Age Stupefies Young Americans and Jeopardizes Our Future (Or, Don't Trust Anyone under 30)*. Ouch.

Millennials, Baby Echoes, Gen Yers, whatever you prefer to call us, are over one-fourth of the U.S. population, born between 1980 and 2000. We have the joystick of America in our well-educated, well-traveled, tech-savvy hands. That seems to put some people on edge. They don't understand us. We grew up playing Mario Kart. They actually went outside.

But there is a key ingredient that those hysterical commentators and concerned parents have missed, a quality that without question separates this enigmatic young generation from all generations prior. (No, not our striking ability to create elaborate emoji tableaux—though those are impressive.) I'm talking about where my generation overwhelmingly spends its money, time, and energy: food.

For the last half-century, young Americans have largely defined themselves by their favorite music and drug of choice as they lean back and listen. Gen Y has shifted the tides. We've swapped guitar strings and lyric books for another form of entertainment and self-expression: cage-free eggs, local cheese and organic kale. If you wanted to pick up a chick in the East Village in the '80s, you walked around with a guitar strapped to your back. Today, you get a tattoo of a carrot on your forearm.

Just call us Generation Yum.

There are roughly 80 million Millennials in America. According to research by ad agency BBDO, half of us call ourselves "foodies." Those 40 million of us are actually not just foodies, we're Yummers. Hey, there (Note: Picture Yummers waving).

Food obsession has infiltrated nearly all sectors of the Millennial generation: younger, older, West Coaster, East Coaster and almost every hungry soul in between.

"The people who really spend a lot of money in restaurants now are the 20-30somethings and they really think of restaurants as an important part of their lives," writer and restaurant reviewer Ruth Reichl told the *Los Angeles Times*. "It's a whole new clientele that has never been part of the American restaurant scene before."

"These young adults put food at the top of the list on how they spend their dollars," Andrew Zimmern, host of the Travel Channel's *Bizarre*

Foods has said. "They know the difference between garganelli and strozzapreti. Across the board, they are three times the gastronauts their parents are."

Yummers grew up in worldly, connected environments, where we learned from movies and classmates that food is not just mac and cheese packets—or whatever we were eating at home—but Indian roti and French baguettes with brie. After the weekend cartoons, Sara Moulton taught us words like "sous vide," "béchamel" and "raita" on The Food Network. Rick Bayless brought Mexican food up from its Taco Bell status during his shows on PBS. Today, recession be damned, we want our single-source coffee and cured meats.

Millennials are more likely to shop at specialty food stores than older generations. In fact, specialty food is among the fastest growing industries in the United States, with sales jumping by 22.1 percent between 2010 and 2012. In 2012, dollar volume for the industry grew an impressive 14.3 percent, bringing in food sales of $85.87 billion, according to the Specialty Food Association. We're also obsessed with everything local, organic and GMO free, supporting the 174 percent rise in farmer's markets from 2000 to 2012. Our tastes are limitless, and our desire to try "exotic" foods, both near and far (ever heard of tangelos?) is encouraging food companies worldwide to revamp their offerings and include unique ingredients like cumin, sriracha and truffles. For the first time ever, teens are spending more on food than clothes.

"Generation Y has a game-changing approach to food consumption that will definitely affect how other demographics, including Gen Xs and Baby Boomers shop and eat," said Kimberly Egan, CEO of the Center for Culinary Development.

This trend isn't just changing the face of fine dining and upscale grocery stores; it is revolutionizing American culture. Fifteen-year-old Caroline Adams has girlfriends over for sleepovers in her parents' St. Louis home where they make pizzas from scratch and allow the dough to rise as they watch a Zac Efron movie and prep homemade pesto. She watches *Chopped*, not *90210*.

Chef Lenny Russo of Minneapolis' Heartland restaurant says that many of his Chef's Table diners (minimum $130 per person) are not old enough to order alcohol. Some call them "foodie savants."

This food fanaticism has seeped into nearly every rank of Millennial populations, and even younger Millennials, those born closer to 2000, now in their early teens, are picking up the fervent obsession with cooking programs, haute ingredients and tasting menus. That means that the 40,000 food blogs, and hundreds of food magazines, food memoirs, cooking reality shows and recipe apps created in the last five years are likely just on the start of an upswing. Hold on to your plates.

Gen Y has been a topic of angst for Boomers ever since they brought us into the world (as all new generations are to their parents, of course). They worry loudly about what we'll do with the power we've been bestowed. We are technologically preoccupied and politically aloof. We practice armchair activism every time we "like" something on Facebook and think we're making a difference. Many take our obsession with food as further evidence of self-indulgent tendencies.

"Foodies Give Me Indigestion," *The Daily Beast* posts. NPR asks, "Are your friends bombarding you with food porn?" "Foodie Backlash Has Come Swiftly, Was Inevitable," reads a headline on *Huffington Post*. The exasperation has even spread overseas. "Let's start the foodie backlash," wrote Steven Poole in *The Guardian* in mid-2012 (an article that was, in fact, just a teaser for his book, *You Aren't What You Eat: Fed Up With Gastroculture*):

> Cookery programmes bloat the television schedules, cookbooks strain the bookshop tables, celebrity chefs hawk their own brands of weird mince pies (Heston Blumenthal) or bronze-moulded pasta (Jamie Oliver) in the supermarkets, and cooks in super-expensive restaurants from Chicago to Copenhagen are the subjects of hagiographic profiles in serious magazines and newspapers. Food festivals (or, if you will, 'Feastivals') are the new rock festivals, featuring thrilling live stage performances of, er, cooking.

I recall opening *New York Magazine* in 2012 to a prominent, colorful spread of food photos with the large title: "When Did Young People Start Spending 25% of Their Paychecks on Pickled Lamb's Tongue?" The article's author, Michael Idov, bashes Yummers, painting us as status crazed, superficial roadies who gawk and photograph every stop on the food love train.

Issues that were once only of concern to chefs, farmers and connoisseurs now find fanatics among the general public, including the inexperienced, younger generation. You can find food trucks in France, for goodness' sake, and over half the Jewish population of Israel tuned in to the 2013 finale of the Israeli edition of cooking reality show *MasterChef*.

But more than anything, Yummer annoyance may come from sheer confusion. Millennials have been handed the keys to America's future, and we're driving our ride straight toward... craft beers, cronuts and David Chang?

What's strangest about this shift is that it happened during one of the worst periods of unemployment and student loan debt in American history. While reading about catastrophic job numbers, we're learning how to make a soufflé and harvest green beans. We must really *love* food if we're spending our few hard-earned bucks (or our parents') on truffle-infused cheese instead of saving up to move out of mom and dad's or buy gas. It belies reality: A generation who graduated or is soon to graduate into a landscape of unemployment and low wages eats out at expensive restaurants more than our Baby Boomer or Gen X counterparts, and purchases organic apples and artisanal bread with money that could have gone to laundry. In July 2014, the unemployment rate of workers under 24 was more than twice the national average. We hear the economy is improving, but we've been hit precisely when we're attempting to begin our professional lives, potentially setting us back for decades.

What's more is that we're also the generation that has, undoubtedly, experienced the greatest access to music ever. Continuing the 50s to 90s teenage obsession with tunes instead of tuna would have been incredibly apt. Napster launched in 1999 and soon other free music sites joined its ranks, like Limewire and Kazaa. Tween and teenage Gen Yers were swimming in free downloads of any musical genre, band, century we wanted to listen to. Yet just a few years after Napster amassed 70 million users, we shut down the application and moved on...to kale salads.

Like so many Millennials, I am obsessed with everything from eating out to the traditions behind and comfort brought by food. I graduated (leaving those microwaved dinners behind) and was immediately thrust into the worst of the recession in 2009. While meandering through a half dozen short-term jobs and three-month stints in various cities, my attention gravitated toward homemade pies, griddled arepas and short-rib tacos.

I have learned to roll sushi and bake Argentine *pão de queijo*. I keep up on the politics around universal composting, and frequently indulge in reruns of *No Reservations* and read memoirs by celebrity chefs. In fact, I have built a career in food, starting with an article about incorporating vegetables into breakfast for *NPR*'s late "Kitchen Window" column, and later as an assistant to *New York Times* food columnist and prolific cookbook author Mark Bittman.

In the years after I graduated Amherst, I noticed the rising profile of Emeril Lagasse and the way people chatted about *Top Chef* at bars. I took note of friends, and then more friends, who started to brew beer at home, some even growing their own hops. I learned that my generation spends 14 times more money on food than an average middle class family, and that 87 percent of us will splurge on a meal even when money is tight. I thought about the choices I was making on a daily basis. Should I really be spending my limited freelance salary on 10-course restaurant meal or pre-made hand rolled pasta instead of factory cut?

Millennials have immense pull on the economy. By 2030, Millennials will likely outnumber Baby Boomers 78 million to 56 million. Baby Boomers will leave $30 trillion to their children over the next 30 to 40 years, on top of the nearly $12 trillion that Boomers will receive from *their* parents. This generation will be (and largely already is) running the American and world economies, with $200 billion in buying power. In fact, by 2017, Millennials are projected to have more spending power than any other generation. U.S. Millennials already account for an estimated $1.3 trillion in direct annual spending. Recession notwithstanding, this generation has money to spend— or will, very soon.

And that money is going toward farmers, wildlife, restaurateurs, distributors and vendors.[i] It's the environment, politics and health wrapped into one—issues that grace the cover of newspapers every day. Ramen has gone from being the 25-cent package staple for college kids to a $25 bowl at Ippudo. Certain dishes (I'm looking at you, pork belly) have become trendy to an extent that may seem bizarre to the outside observer; what were once considered exotic ingredients are garnering devoted mainstream audiences. Kids with top college degrees are applying their learning to harvests instead of hedge funds. And certain products, like quinoa, acai and kale, have become the shining badge of "foodie" eaters.

A concern for what's in our food has been an oscillating trend in American history, from Sylvester Graham preaching about whole wheat in 1830 to fears of DDT and world hunger in the late 1960s. But the macro situation never really changed. Today, it is. Labels boast *local* and *organic*; menus list ingredient origins; and gardening is being introduced into some urban schools. There is, without a doubt, a ripple effect when 55 percent of America's youth are willing to spend more to get top quality ingredients.

This, of course, is great news, as we are currently battling some pretty big issues, among them global warming, obesity and feeding an overpopulated planet. Yummers are bringing others into the fold of organic eating, composting, breaking down recipes and building them up. I know I certainly *feel* righteous every time I purchase vitamin-rich, locally grown, non-GMO, organic kale.

Yet the media love to point out that our interest also has a dark side: Food has become a social currency that we use to test others' culinary wherewithal. Have you eaten at that four-star restaurant; had that famous chef's award winning dish; traveled to wherever to try that local delicacy?

Millennials are now the largest generation on earth. Commentators lament the impact of technology on our childhood development, economists reveal this generation's record-breaking unemployment levels, and others simply make fun of us, but they're not bothering to investigate the *why* behind our obsession with food.

The legacy of the Millennial generation is just now being written. As those born between 1980 and 2000 begin to leave home, the world is shifting with their impact. From the development of Facebook by Mark Zuckerberg, born in 1984, to Jon Favreau—the former Millennial speechwriter for the President—, Generation Yum holds sway in the ever-quickening world. We're spending on new things. We seem to value experiences more than commodities, making marketers scramble as they reevaluate how to woo this "do" versus "have" generation. Businesses grow as Kickstarter helps teenagers fund projects and social media provide free promotional tools. We have upended the publishing world with blogs, television with YouTube, modes of public transportation with Lyft, travel with Trevolta and concepts of privacy with social media familiarity. Open a newspaper and some person in my generation is making headlines. Generation Yum is the next round of powerful wave makers.

Several years after college I was living in New York, working as a food writer. I found an apartment I could afford in Park Slope, one of the most popular neighborhoods in Brooklyn. Trouble was, the apartment was only 250 square feet—closets and bathroom included. I could fit a full sized bed, a mini desk, loveseat, small high-top table with four stools and that was about it. The kitchen consisted of a sink, mini fridge under four burners and a microwave oven. I could touch both sides of the kitchen at the same time, wall to wall, if I reached out my arms, Titanic style. I joked that cleaning the apartment was a snap. I'd stand in one spot and move my Swiffer in a fan-like shape, and I was done.

Still, I cooked all the time. To make space to chop, I'd slide an oversized wood block on top of the sink, under the faucet. When I had to get some water, I'd move the block to the high top behind me. It became a well-choreographed dance.

Some nights, I'd come home several drinks in and starved. In my buzzed and drowsy state, I'd weigh my options: order in or cook. Most of the time, I slid out my chopping block and made a meal from whatever I had on hand. Canned tomatoes and chickpeas, a couple sweet potatoes and a zucchini would transform into a Moroccan harissa stew.

One evening, after a day of photographing and testing several recipes for an NPR article, I invited three friends over to help me eat the results. As I finished prepping what remained of the meal, my friends sat on the loveseat and watched as I moved my chopping block back and forth, washing and chopping intermittently, going up and down a stepping stool to stir the yellow lamb curry bubbling on the stovetop, as the burners were too high for me to see into the pot from the floor.

"Where do you do the dishes?" my friend asked. "In the bathtub?"

It was hilarious not just to think of scrubbing a plate and myself Kramer-style, but even more so because his question was genuine. It was ridiculous that I bothered to cook there. No person in her right mind would. But I had to. It was my way to unwind. Food had become the center of my existence: I researched restaurants to go to with friends, exchanged recipes, watched cooking shows, read cookbooks. At some point I had to wonder: How did this happen? Why was food suddenly so enticing when back at Amherst I couldn't give two hoots what I was eating?

Years after food had become integral to my social, creative and working worlds, I found myself confused and curious. I wanted to sit my generation on the therapist's couch. I wanted to know why I find *Iron Chef America* so entrancing, as the chefs race to produce food that I cannot taste or smell and am unlikely to reproduce at home; why high schools now integrate food sections in their newspapers; why we tweet photos of our lunches to strangers. For that matter, why do we bother to look at photos of lunches eaten by strangers? Why do we care about Korean taco trucks or farmers markets when most of us don't have the extra money to spend? Why is my friend with a degree from UCLA ditching the world of consulting to make grilled cheese?

In restaurants, I watch as patrons hold their iPhones high to find the optimal angle to photograph a bubbling hot pot or melting panino. I listen to friends discuss their last great meal. New concerns emerge every day regarding what we eat, where we eat it and how it is grown.

Brushing off this cultural shift as a "fad," that, like pet rocks, will slowly fade from popularity, misinterprets the sincerity and gravity of this movement. Answers to global concerns around Gen Yum lie within our interactions with food: our decisions to leave work and meet friends at a restaurant we spent hours researching, or head home to bake bread from scratch, or make a career change that leaves our florescent lighted offices for something in the sun.

There are, of course, exceptions. If you went in search of acai in most communities in the U.S., you would receive looks suggesting your lunacy, and for good reason. The United States food system is fraught with inconsistencies, biases and insufficient foodways. A child who grows up in a food desert is far less likely to have access to (or interest in) the Cooking Channel or locally-butchered prosciutto or feel, for that matter, that extra effort or money should be put toward organic versus factory produced. Economics and education play an enormous role in creating and maintaining sustainable food systems throughout the country.

That said, the majority of U.S. Millennials (nearly six in 10) grew up in upper-middle-class or wealthy families. (To put things in perspective, about six in 10 Boomers grew up in middle or low-income families.) Almost half of us will inherit money from our parents. Recessionary fears aside, we are, by and large, very privileged, and this segment of the generation is already leading the world with its opinions and dollars. This vocal and influential section of this generation cares about food, for reasons I am eager to explore. With their kombucha kits, windowsill hydroponic garden and Anthropology rolling pins, they are what I call Generation Yum.

We are the guinea pigs for the foreseeable future. Unlike any generation that ever was or ever will be, we have straddled the technology boom. Those of us born in the '80s and early '90s didn't grow up with cell phones or laptops. We mainly did research papers in the library using the Dewey Decimal system. If we needed directions, we pulled out a paper map. We called friends on the (landline) phone and arranged in-person dates. We couldn't cancel last minute by sending a text; we had to actually show up. We bought CDs and, before that, cassettes. No one was concerned with organic or fair-trade or local. And we've watched as all that has changed.

Over the last many years, I have compiled articles about food and community, food trends, food history, sociology and food, psychology and food, printed each article, stapled and hole punched, clipped and underlined before alphabetically arranging them in a binder I fear is reaching the weight of my young nephew.

I've hung my head in shame, gawked at startling statistics, and been drawn into the complicated, political history of food. I determined that even if this Gen Yum food "craze" is indeed just that (though I'm quite sure it's not), it's a well-needed one. There is a gap, a big one, that food is filling, and I'm not just referring to our stomachs (although it is worth mentioning that, paralleling the rise in food culture, the percent of obese adults more than doubled between 1980 and 2000, jumping from 13 percent to 28 percent among men and from 17 percent to 34 percent among women. Just tuck that factoid away for later.). In a land of over-stimulation, over-consumption, we are, in many ways, a malnourished generation.

Taste, smell, chop, lick, savor, indulge, cut, burn, bleed, fry, sizzle, pop. That friend who always knows the latest restaurants, who snaps a photo of each meal, who ooos and ahhs over burrata, has a reason to be so scintillated and so satisfied. The same goes for those who after a long day at the office or studying hard at school, return home to craft their own tapenade, bake vegan cookies or prepare an extravagant meal, sometimes just for themselves. And ditto for the friend who graduated from college and instead of chasing after those increasingly elusive jobs with healthcare benefits, ended up harvesting clams or milking goats or tilling the land. These choices are increasingly common: Young people are actively, purposefully integrating food into their lives and giving it daily attention—and value—in a different proportion than any previous generation.

This book will suggest that these are not trends but statements of values that are likely to endure as Yummers age. I will try to explain what needs are being met in a cooking class or dinner club or zucchini field. I will walk you through my own journey, through interviews with young Americans around the country who follow restaurant trends, read cookbooks in bed, and have left corporate jobs for a life with their hands in the soil. I will also introduce you to the leaders of the food movement in America, the names that fill the pages of *The New York Times* or *Lucky Peach* and inform us about the latest news in agriculture, restaurants or cooking innovations: Anthony Bourdain, Michael Pollan, Mark Bittman, Francis Lam, Peter Meehan, Marion Nestle, Ken Friedman, Rick Bayless, Greil Marcus and more.

I started investigating Generation Yum to better understand myself and my peers, to pin down where our interest in food comes from and uncover some indications of where it will lead future generations. What could I discover about my generation's impact on politics, the economy and social issues through our decisions in food? I was ready to ignore the naysayers and take a good hard look at what makes us tick.

Critics label this generation lazy and entitled without asking us why we do the things we do. In some ways, we're totally average, but the fact that the greatest rise in Millennial spending is projected to be on fresh fruits, organic food and natural cleaning products (hugely beating out sodas, apps or luxury brands) is truly exceptional. That is something to note, something to investigate, something to attempt to understand. Which is exactly what I aim to do in this book. Join me, as I attempt to figure out my own generation, and along the way, a little bit about myself.

Chapter 1
Bye, Mom and Dad, I'm Going Out For Dinner

On a snowy New York afternoon, up on the 12th floor of a high rise in Hell's Kitchen, I swung my chair around to face my editor for a quick meeting. During a spell of (f)unemployment, I'd decided to take a part time editorial gig in the Food and Drink section of a well-known New York magazine.

"We're assigning you a new feature for Valentine's Day," my editor said, slowly rolling her eyes and exhaling, speaking as though she just. couldn't. even. I grabbed a pen and paper to scribble down some notes. "The idea is panty droppers for foodies," she stated.

My pen paused. "Panty droppers?"

"We want things that, like, foodies would, like, panty drop over," she said with a Valley Girl twang, hands flying in the air to indicate, 'Ya *know*? Duh.'

"What does that *mean*?" My mother later asked me over the phone as I explained my latest task.

"I think it means find restaurant dishes that turn people on," I said.

"People are turned on by food?"

"I think it's supposed to be funny," I offered, attempting to rationalize the assignment. But I knew it was absurd. When I turned in the piece, I received editorial comments like, "Add [redacted restaurant name]'s chickpea fritters which are slightly phallic since they're in a cigar shape."

But what was clear, no matter how outrageous the assignment, was that food's reputation had changed. Find foods that people want to do, that turn them on, that excite them. The truth is that there isn't anything much more fashionable or sexy in New York than knowing the best restaurants. And this is a trend reverberating around the United States, the overseas even.

What Recession?

"A lot of people really like eating out. It's a badge of pride to call yourself a foodie, to have good taste." Cliff Chang is a computer software engineer at Asana, a San Francisco Bay startup. Chang is 26, originally from outside Chicago. He wears his dark hair cropped short, and, in Chuck

Taylors, jeans and a t-shirt, he fits the prevailing fashion of Silicon Valley. He's not what fifty years ago—heck, ten years ago—anyone would have imagined as the average restaurant enthusiast, a dining devotee. He is a former Facebook Transmedia Architect (I won't pretend to know what that means) and Computer Science major at the California Institute of Technology in Pasadena. He spends his time "being a nerd, generally," and lives with three roommates who also work in the computer world. Cliff doesn't cook; his kitchen is "super tiny." But he can definitely tell you where to eat.

Dosas, burritos, "authentic" Chinese—Cliff's got you covered. He knows about the once-a-week "pop-ups," during which an ephemeral restaurant (often open for a week or two, sometimes one night only) takes over the kitchen of a permanent one. He follows food carts and trucks on Twitter, including the Pizza Hacker, a retired software engineer who bakes pizza at home and sells from a cart, Tweeting at his fans where and when to come buy a slice. (I picture computer programmers in hoodies pulling out their earbuds and darting out the door to beat the rest of the nerdy horde to the steaming, bubbling slices.) "Best damn pizza in the city," Cliff states with confidence. And I believe him. He knows about every restaurant opening in his neighborhood. He has spent $270 for a prix fixe meal at The French Laundry, widely regarded as one of the finest restaurants in the world, synonymous with the best seasonal, regional ingredients.

"Most of my friends are not that into food. Well, hold on," Chang pauses. He had spent the last forty minutes telling me about San Francisco's food obsession, the young computer engineers in his office who spar over where to find the best barbecue in Austin or which ice-cream shop offers the best frosty treat. And don't get him started on the taquerias. "Everyone's got pretty strong opinions about which taqueria is the best. Even though, I don't really know. I like eating burritos, they're tasty… but none of us know what an authentic taco is anyway."

Why *do* they care? Why will Cliff, a self-described nerd from the Midwest, wait in line for over an hour for brunch? Why do other young San Franciscans line up before dawn at Tartine Bakery to get the oven fresh pastries? Cliff blames it on the money available to these family-less Internet moguls, him included. While others may have bought a car or home, Cliff lives with his roommates in a shared apartment and spends his extra cash on fantastic eats. But does that explain the constant food conversations? The endless Yelping? (Some restaurants in San Francisco, Yelp's hometown, have over 5,000 reviews.) And the behavior that Cliff describes—eagerly awaiting restaurant openings, arguing over where to find the best of the best, eating both at high-end restaurants and searching for the best cheap grub—is not a Silicon Valley trend. It's a nation-wide epidemic.

Young America is taking on an interest that used to be considered highfalutin'. But why? Shouldn't we be going to concerts or museums, jumping up and down to loud music and taking drugs or at least attempting something illegal? Why should we care if Eddie Huang's pork bun is juicier than David Chang's?

But Cliff does. He reads message boards to see what restaurants are opening and on weekends travels to find the best eats in the city. And this interest is spiking during a time when fewer young people have the means to buy a home or host a wedding, let alone a nice dinner. Most of us are not like Cliff. We don't have the option of buying a car, playing a round of golf each week, or even joining a gym. But many share Cliff's culinary habits nonetheless. In fact, 42 percent of Millennials eat at a fine dining restaurant at least once a month, which is twice the rate for our beloved parents, the Baby Boomers. In fact, we eat out in general—be it five course menus or a handful of doner kebab—more than any other age group. Times are a changin'.

Before I moved to New York, I lived and worked in Washington, D.C., first as a Communications Research Assistant at a think tank, then as a waitress. This may seem backwards, but it wasn't to me.

After graduating, I fell into the funk of recessionary times. To escape, I packed my bags and, in a moment of either sheer genius or dumb luck, decided to move to Argentina to live on the peso. I wrote for an expat paper and toured glaciers, rivers, and vineyard rows in South America. For the first time I was writing about food: I reviewed a bagel shop, a bike and wine tour, and a cooking class. My most memorable experiences happened around the table—sharing glasses of Malbec, plates of crunchy mullejas and chichulines, or seared steaks with the table full of condiments. After three months down south, I found a job back in the States and returned home.

I researched and wrote about unemployment and underemployment and floated in post-graduate agony, clueless of where to take my life next. I'd wake up each morning at the same hour, walk to the train behind others dressed just like me, and spend my day in a windowless hallway behind a cubicle partition, staring at my computer screen. While some of the work was interesting, most of it wasn't, and I missed working in food. I began writing for NPR freelance, covering food history and developing recipes. At the time, I had no real credentials to my name beyond the few articles I'd published in Buenos Aires, but I did have a passionate interest. Seven months later, I decided to quit my full time job and apply for a Masters in writing. I'd save up money by waitressing.

I landed at a new Spanish restaurant in Northwest D.C. It was just what many locals were clamoring for: upscale shared plates in a cozy setting, and exotic foods like blistered shishito peppers and charred squid with romesco.

In 2010, the food scene in D.C. was still nascent. Locals ate at chains like Buca di Beppo and Five Guys, and the only major chef to have made significant headway was José Andrés, with his restaurants Jaleo and Oyamel. But investors and chefs were noticing Andrés' success and wanting in. Young government workers, it seemed, were willing to pay fifty dollars or more for dinner, even on their limited budgets. This was something new.

"Some of the country's best and most famous chefs are eschewing New York and other big U.S. cities to open restaurants in Washington," reported the *Washington Times* in 2011, "driven in large part by young professionals."

"They are the ones that want to experience good food," chef and *Top Chef* contestant Mike Isabella told the paper.

Back in 2010, *The Washington Post* reported the surging demand for gourmet eats, craft beers and no attitude dining, calling the trend "the New York-ification of the D.C. food scene."

Four nights a week I would mount my secondhand red and rusty bicycle and pedal downhill from my shared, converted one-to-two bedroom apartment in Cleveland Park to the gentrifying neighborhood just south of U Street. Dressed in my mandated uniform of Chuck Taylors, jeans, and a custom black t-shirt, I would clean and set tables and memorize the updated menu before the doors opened and young patrons rushed in, often still dressed in their gray professional wear.

My favorite part of the job was the tastings. The menu featured a number of unique ingredients that just a few years previous you'd be hard-pressed to find in D.C. One night a month, the staff would gather at the back bar after service, beginning around midnight, to taste samples of pungent

Spanish cheeses, cured meats, Midwestern craft beers, and $300 bottles of Rioja wines that our managers hoped we could sell.

And we did. Patrons would settle into their wide, leather and wooden seats and escape to Spain. Rustic chandeliers, slate tile floors, metal lined counter-tops and top-end international treats like Garrotxa cheese, *porrones* of Txacoli and hot *morcilla* sausages wooed eaters into a trance. I watched as their demeanors shifted. Everything that had made me uncomfortable with my former desk job was absent—the diners weren't talking business. Their phones were put away. This was all before the popularity of Instagram (which launched that year, in October), before food porn had truly taken off, and the restaurant served as a respite from the 24-hour news cycle in exchange for human and sensory connection. Some went into the bathroom and literally let down their hair before ordering one more glass of Tempranillo. The buttoned-up Washington workers squashed around the bar as they waited to be seated, sometimes for up to two hours, and crowded around community tables where they shared recommendations on what to order next. It was like they walked through the restaurant door and suddenly, everything was ok.

Dinnertime has changed. Twentysomethings spend hours thinking about a meal before we go out, indulging from appetizer to dessert. Later, we evaluate the meal online, bequeathing (or not) yellow stars on Yelp, OpenTable or Zagat, with our reflections on a favorite cocktail or the careless hostess. It doesn't matter if it's a $150 meal at a top-end joint or $2 dumplings off a cart. It's an evening's activity. Forget the show; let's just go to dinner.

In the widely read *New York Magazine* article "When Did Young People Start Spending 25% of Their Paychecks on Pickled Lamb's Tongue?" Michael Idov writes:

> One of the main hallmarks of twentysomething life… has typically been to not give a shit what and where you eat. As recently as the late nineties, a steady diet of burritos and takeout Chinese… was part of the Generation X ethic. An abiding interest in food was something for old people or snobs, like golf or opera. The notion of idolizing chefs, filling notebooks with restaurant 'life lists,' or talking about candied foie gras on a date was out-and-out bizarre. Lately, however, food has become a defining obsession among a wide swath of the young and urbane.

It *is* cool to eat out, to know about the latest restaurant opening, the superstar chefs. And it's not bizarre behavior, at least to us. But Idov is on to something: It should be, right?

Our interest in restaurants is a particularly shocking trend for a generation that has been body slammed by the economic downturn. Since 2010, the number of working young adults has been at its lowest since the government began keeping track in 1948. That means we are the least employed group of young people in the last 60 years.[ii] In 2010, only 54.3 percent of young adults were employed. By January 2013, the numbers had risen to 62.9 percent working, but half only part-time. The unemployment rate for those 16 to 24 is still twice the national rate.

To make things worse, recessionary times have been particularly hard on new worker income. Full-time employed young adults have seen their weekly earnings drop by 6 percent, more than any other age group. And more income is shaved away when you factor in the $1 trillion owed in outstanding student loan debt, the highest amount ever. The Federal Reserve Bank of New York reports that Americans now owe more in student loans than on credit cards. Millennials are so broke they're moving back in with mom and dad, and postponing marriage and home ownership. Economically speaking, things are in the dumps for Generation Y.[iii]

But who cares? Let's go get a burger. I know a great place.

In New York City, some of the most in-demand tables are owned by Ken Friedman, a forty-something ex-music mogul who, with cash to spare and a desire for something new, decided to hop on the restaurant wagon and open a few joints in the Big Apple. I met him at the Breslin, one of his most successful ventures, known for its hip scene and pork fried peanuts (just seven bucks a pop).

The Breslin is housed in the Ace Hotel at the intersection of West 29th and Broadway. It's a bit of no man's land, sandwiched between the high-end stores north of Union Square and the bustling chaos of Korea Town. Neighbored by wig shops and tables of counterfeit jewelry, the upscale hotel sits next to another Friedman restaurant, the John Dory. The lobby holds the Ace Hotel's own bar and a Stumptown Coffee cafe, always full of twentysomethings squished into the small space to get in line for the pricey, potent brew. If you want to settle in, feel free. You can take your piping hot, direct trade, responsibly sourced, often organic coffee and recline in the dimly lit lobby filled with mismatched couches and tables of different heights and lengths, assembled in circles and squares in the vast space. You can also order from the lobby bar. A beer may be $12, but the wifi is free.

As Friedman and I scooched into his designated booth at the far end of the Breslin—outfitted with computer plugs, chargers and a light-up button to call the waitress—he revealed the genius of the hotel's location: close to cheap office space (or as cheap as you'll find in Manhattan). Friedman dubs the area "Silicon Alley," filled with "all these young people with these techie ideas," who don't have tons of money and spend their days in front of computers in cramped workspaces (that is, people like Cliff but without the large, comped company cafeteria or meal stipend). The hotel was constructed in part to get these young tech guys and gals out of their isolated digital worlds and into a communal space.

Walk into the Ace lobby and you'll see a light display of shining screens illuminating the faces of diligent workers in the low-lit lounge, their work spread out on rustic wooden tables, feet resting on fuzzy cushions or rugs. To get out of their "shitty little offices," as Friedman put it, these workers, who spend all day online regardless, now sit in the lobby and "buy food, they'll drink coffee, they'll get beer." Then, when they want a break, they walk through a doorway into The Breslin.

The dining room's faux rustic design evokes down-home Midwestern America: a mishmash of "antique" tchotchkes and rural chic decor. Friedman says it's supposed to be reminiscent of a London pub. Brown paper covers the booth counters and long communal tables. The menu is heavy on meat-focused plates: chargrilled lamb burger with feta, cumin mayo and thrice cooked chips; pig's foot for two with creamy shallots and fried Brussels sprouts. Sides include market beans with tomato and nigella, pumpkin with buttermilk and crispy sage, roasted Brussels sprouts with apple, roasted cauliflower with Szechuan peppercorns. Beers, including a custom cask brew made by neighboring craft brewery Six Point, go for ten bucks each. You can eat until your cholesterol hits the roof, you have a healthy buzz, and your wallet is empty, which won't take long.

It's often difficult to secure a table at the no reservations restaurant. Young scruffy folks with thick-framed glasses linger over a beer or a burger. And they keep coming back. I asked Ken for his secret, how he has been able to conjure up lines of avid young fans at nearly all of his restaurant locations.

He leaned in and placed his hands in a triangle, fingertips touching. I felt like I was about to be privy to important information.

Friedman said the Spotted Pig, another of his local spots, is set up specifically to create a community space. Tables are close to one another and stools are missing backs. The uncomfortable seating forces diners to lean in. The mix of condensed personal bubbles, hearty food, dim lighting and communal dining arrangements ensure that intimate conversation is always on the menu. Once, Friedman said, he overheard a patron on the phone saying, "I've made more friends at The Spotted Pig than all throughout high school and college combined."

"And I loved that," Friedman exclaimed, his hands rising in excitement. "I got goosebumps from that. 'Cause you sit there at the Pig, and you can't help but be like, 'Oo, what's that' and, 'Taste that,' and you make friends." Friedman points around the table at invisible dishes, and smiles. He has, in short, created the antithesis to the office cubicle: no borders, boundaries, screens or headphones. What you get is real people, real food, real noise and intoxicating smells. Patrons arrive in jeans and t-shirts but the menu is first class. It's casual enough to feel comfortable, but upscale enough that you don't feel like an idiot for spending $35 on lunch. It's the comforts of home with an all-star chef. And The Breslin follows the same rubric.

Now, take a moment and think of the latest hip restaurant opening in your town. Chances are it sounds a lot like the The Spotted Pig. Restaurants around the country are offering communal tables, communal meals. Strangers gather to share drinks and even reach out their forks or chopsticks to taste each other's food. While living in Washington, D.C., I joked with my friends about the number of "tapas" joints: Greek "tapas," Mexican "tapas," Turkish "tapas." *Tapas, people,* I wanted to say, *are just Spanish!* But at 5:00pm, the D.C. office junkies gather, drink their grappa or margaritas or Turkish wine and nosh with friends on the ever-expanding list of small plate options. The setup encourages conversation and group outings. In some cases, it makes the meal more affordable. In others, it makes it a bill worth paying, an experience worth having.

Gen Y has created a "sharing economy," with shared car, housing, and even shared clothing programs, almost all of which are arranged via app or online. Ride around San Francisco and you'll likely notice cars sporting bright pink mustaches. These are drivers participating in Lyft, a ride share program. Craigslist provides a platform for everything under the sun: a new couch, a research assistant, a cross-country ride from New York to L.A. Housing is no exception. We're staying in each other's homes with the help of Airbnb and Couchsurfing. We use these services to save us cash *except* when it comes to food, the one area, it seems, where we're actually willing to spend *more* for a unique experience, even when it's shared.[iv]

And this constant sharing is rocking the economy as we shy away from buying homes and cars and instead devote a larger percentage of our income to food and travel. Material commodities are out; experience is in.

Underground dinner parties and their ilk are finding success now for a reason. Young people are choosing new ways to spend their money. Shared housing while traveling? Not an issue. Public transportation? I'm game. $100 for a meal to which I have to bring my own booze but I get to meet interesting people and chill in someone's house for the night? Sounds like a plan.

Comfort food is another element that makes the Breslin and similar restaurants feel so damn cozy. All around the country, riffs on old home-cooked meals are bringing in diners: Poco's lobster mac n' cheese in New York, L.A.'s Flying Pig food truck's duck confit tacos, Philly's gourmet dogs at Hot Diggity, Cincinnati startup Tom+Chee's grilled cheese and tomato soup mashups and Las Paletas Gourmet Popsicles in Nashville. If a mom seems to be in the kitchen cooking, the Yummers will come.

Kappo: Served in the Kitchen

We're looking for comfort wherever we can find it. Many of the up-and-coming restaurants include open kitchens or windows so that visitors can see into the prep areas, merging the worlds of cooks and diners. A conversation can take place, actually or emotionally, between the patron and the provider. This is a concept that in the old world of fine dining would have seemed outright uncouth. The kitchen was something to be hidden. Today, it's the way we welcome each other in. We can even see this in home design, with a growing preference for "open concept" kitchen and living room layouts where kitchens are merged with the hang-out areas.

Diners want to watch the chef expertly chop an onion or sear a skewer of yakitori. It adds closeness to the dining experience usually only found at home, on reality television, or around a campfire. That is, until now.

One of the latest trends is *kappo* dining, a Japanese tradition started in the 19th century, where elevated cuisine is served *in* the kitchen, chef and customer face to face. As a dish is finished, it is handed over the bar directly to the customer. Several restaurants around the world are beginning to incorporate this method of chef and diner interaction, including Chef's Table at Brooklyn Fare, Atera, Blanca, Momofuku Ko, and Kappo at Má Pêche in New York City; Miyabi's "modern kappo" in Honolulu; Sushi Kappo Tamura in Seattle; and Water Library Thonglor in Bangkok.

"What's most important in kappo," Masaaki Nakamura, chef of Osaka's Wayoyuzen Nakamura is reported saying in *The Wall Street Journal*, "is the relationship between the chef and the diners. It should be casual and conversational, even when we are making the most complex cuisine."

Open kitchens go "hand in hand with the celebrity chef," 29-year-old Washington, D.C. executive chef Marjorie Meek-Bradley says. "If you watch [chefs] on TV, it's even better to watch them live."

This trend also follows suit with the booming attention paid to "dining clubs." Meetup.com, a site dedicated to organizing local groups with similar interests—from fly fishing to chess to Malaysian cuisine—received so many requests for dinner meetups that they began Dinner.Meetup.com, exclusively dedicated to those looking for like-minded gourmands. The site runs in 96 cities in 14 countries, with Australia, Canada, and United Arab Emirates as the top country participants. Clubs like the Gastronauts go out together in search of the most exotic cuisine in New York, Los Angeles and Washington D.C. There are groups for those who love pork, those who love curry. Some meet in local restaurants and others in members' homes. Dining clubs are the new book clubs, the place to go to meet new people and share an intimate experience. There's even Eat With, where you sign up for meals cooked in stranger's homes. The company pairs curious diners with open-minded home-cooks in cities around the world, from Amsterdam to Tel Aviv. These *kappo* meals focus on the ingredients and the cooks preparing the dishes, especially when the meal is held in someone's home.

Kitchensurfing, which launched in New York and Kitchit, from San Francisco, are two new sites helping diners stay close to the kitchen, bringing all-star chefs right to your home. No need to leave the comforts of your own space, just bring the talented chef and top-end ingredients to your stovetop. Basically, it's rent-a-chef, for anywhere from one night to one month. It's a way to have a gathering at your home with friends but still eat a gourmet meal.

"Millennials visit restaurants more frequently than any other generation," says Darren Tristano, the executive vice president of Technomic, a food industry consulting firm. "Success with today's Millennial consumer will depend on making an emotional connection."

Dine, Lick, Click

It's strange that in a time of unprecedented technological advances, eating, that most basic of human necessities, is what's hip. Then again, maybe it makes perfect sense that in a tech-infused world, a craving for intimacy— exactly the feeling produced at Ken Friedman's restaurants—would emerge. Our social landscape has changed drastically in the last decade. Our news is no longer held and turned, but buffered and scrolled; home movies are not only watched with loved ones but blasted out to relatives around the world, and sometimes strangers too. We show support for an idea or project by "liking" it, instead of foot-out-the-door action.[v]

As we type, click, and swipe our lives away, there are, without a doubt, repercussions. This generation grew up alongside the Y2K technological boom, and the youngest of the Yummers, who are just now jumping from middle to high school, have been symbiotic with machines from the get-go. We don't have to think through keyboard shortcuts—our fingertips have them memorized.

Toddlers swipe at iPad screens and mentally leave the room to dive into their own virtual worlds. Families are spending less time together. In June 2009, researchers at the Center for the Digital Future at the University of Southern California's Annenberg School for Communication released a report showing the "erosion of face-to-face family time, increased feelings of being ignored by family members using the Web, and growing concerns that children are spending too much time online." The number of people claiming to spend less time with their siblings, parents or children since installing an Internet connection has nearly tripled, going from 11 percent in 2006, to 28 percent in 2008. 74.8 percent of American households have Internet at home. As smartphones, e-readers and a bevy of new devices begin to inhabit our lives, time spent together will inevitably continue to diminish.

I have seen my own habits shift. It's hard to break away from the shiny screens and guilty-pleasure TV shows with Twitter feeds scrolling across the bottom. Researcher Amber Case, a cyborg anthropologist (yes, that's apparently a real thing), believes we are slowly becoming, well, robots—our devices as critical as our limbs. She claims that "we now rely on 'external brains' (cell phones and computers) to communicate, remember, even live out secondary lives." Extreme, maybe, but it also rings true.[vi]

I've searched for jobs, applied, been interviewed, hired, worked and quit a job all online, without ever meeting my employer. And we lived in the same city. As soon as I wake in the morning, I reach for my cell phone and scan through my emails and the latest news. I am staring at a screen from dawn to dusk. I am so glued to my phone I feel phantom vibrations and hear false ringing, thinking I have an incoming call or text. I'm too ashamed to actually calculate the hours I spend online, doing everything from working to chatting with friends to purchasing home goods, stalking ex-boyfriends, and browsing headlines.

And I am not alone. Facebook has over one billion users. Currently, 85 percent of Millennials own a smartphone and spend over 14 hours per week staring at the illuminated screens. 58 percent of that group admits that they can't go one hour without checking their phones. 90 percent of four-year college students and 80 percent of all 18-to-29 year-olds have a Facebook account. Twitter has over 271 million monthly, active users. While the majority of social networkers are between the ages of 25 and 34, users ages 18 to 24 are more likely to be on YouTube, Twitter, Instagram and Tumblr. We are always plugged in, sharing our thoughts and hopes, and sometimes mistakes, which will live (possibly, see footnote) forever in the digital afterlife.[vii] We post videos of ourselves and provide intimate details on dating sites. We look up health symptoms on WebMD and post restaurant dish recommendations. We take a digital stroll through a neighborhood we'll visit on an upcoming trip. We find recipes, of course. We shop and play. We find others with similar interests and form groups.

Technology, due to its complete infiltration in our lives, continues to build in importance. In 2014, The Bank of America Trends in Consumer Mobility report found that Millennials say their smartphones are more important to them than deodorant or toothpaste. (Others around them would probably argue otherwise.) Another study (commissioned by Zipcar) shows that almost 40 percent of Millennials believe that losing their phones would be worse than losing their cars, and 46 percent of 18-to-24 year olds choose access to the Internet over access to their own car.[viii] Suddenly "Dude, Where's My Car?" holds far less weight.[ix] Answer: "Who Cares? Where's Your Phone?"

The thing is, many users would admit that these online connections are not as meaningful as in-person interactions, and the superficial sense of community they create only leaves participants wanting the real thing. And restaurant owners like Ken Friedman have begun to figure this out.

You Love Your iPhone, But It Can't Love You Back

Is something profound unfolding when a computer-strapped worker in the Ace Hotel lobby snaps her laptop closed and ventures over to the Breslin for a meal? Today, most Americans are almost always connected to some device, especially those under 35. That is, until we go out to dine. There, according to a study by Lookout, young people use their phones less than their Gen X counterparts. We stash them away and give the stink eye to those who spend dinner texting—or, God forbid, having a loud one-sided conversation (or "halfalogue" as its been dubbed). While we certainly whip out our phones for the obligatory money shot, devices are often banished for the remaining meal—and even those seconds of technological interruption are beginning to meet judgmental scorn.[x] Some restaurants are insisting that our shiny palm attachments be put away: Momofuku Ko and Brooklyn Fare have forbidden people from photographing their food. Face-to-face time is being reclaimed.

"We are tempted to think that our little 'sips' of online connection add up to a big gulp of real conversation. But they don't," writes Sherry Turkle, Professor of the Social Studies of Science and Technology at MIT, in her *New York Times* op-ed "The Flight From Conversation." Turkle says our online existence is keeping us from in-person connection and the hours spent G-chatting give us the false feeling of intimacy. "We've become accustomed to a new way of being 'alone together,'" writes Turkle, arguing that our full attention is rarely on the people or events around us. We communicate in snippets of edited text, replying when it's most convenient. We never truly demand one another's attention or care; we're happy to give and receive it whenever we have the moment to hit send.

"We often use technology to save time," writes Jonathan Safran Foer in a *New York Times* op-ed, "but increasingly, it either takes the saved time along with it, or makes the saved time less present, intimate and rich. I worry that the closer the world gets to our fingertips, the further it gets from our hearts. It's not an either/or—being 'anti-technology' is perhaps the only thing more foolish than being unquestioningly 'pro-technology'—but a question of balance that our lives hang upon."

In his book *The Shallows: What the Internet Is Doing to Our Brains*, Nicholas Carr writes: "The price we pay to assume technology's power is alienation." Our persistent technological connections "numb the most intimate, the most human, of our natural capacities—those for reason, perception, memory, emotion…While this cybernetic blurring of mind and machine may allow us to carry out certain cognitive tasks far more efficiently, it poses a threat to our integrity as human beings."

Millennials are beginning to show signs of technology withdrawal, or at the very least, an understanding of how distracted these technologies make us. In Silicon Valley, some young workers play "phone stack," where they place their phones in the middle of the conference table during a meeting. The first to reach for his or her phone buys everyone lunch.

"Computers are really crazy," Chris Muscarella, a 30-year-old web developer and restaurant owner, told me one afternoon over coffee in Cobble Hill, Brooklyn. Chris made his money in the computer world, working at the dot com CUseeMe and then spent three and half years building Mobile Commons, a company that facilitates mobile messaging campaigns (which you may have seen raising money for Haiti or the Red Cross, or in the midst of the SOPA/PIPA controversy). But eventually he took that money and opened Rucola, a rustic Italian restaurant in Brooklyn, and later, Kitchensurfing, bringing chefs into homes for events or cooking demonstrations.

"You've been dealing with a very abstract kind of logic all day long that's so far removed from an emotional connection to a person, or being able to tell a story, or laugh at a joke," Chris says about coding. "When you really get in the zone, you're in that zone for ten, twelve, sixteen hours at a pop. At the end of that period of time, when you kind of come out of that, you're incapable of having a good interaction with another person. There was a sense when we first opened the restaurant that it was like therapy," he told me, explaining the mindset shift required to play host after a day of writing code. This change, Chris tells me "somehow all of a sudden made everything better. It was like, 'Oh, back to being a person again. This is really cool.'"

The research on the relationship between social media and loneliness is clear. Spending time online often isolates us; it amplifies depression and jealousy and lowers our self-esteem. This, I do not find shocking. I'm not sure about you, but sometimes I feel the pull of envy after looking at friends' photos on Facebook. Everyone's lives just seem so damn perfect. I need to remind myself that it's a carefully curated front. Then again, the Internet can be a powerful supporter of one's self-esteem and happiness if you use it the right way, invaluable when coordinating an outing or a meal with friends. Problems arise when we begin to rely on our avatar relationships over our actual ones.[xi]

We have become emotionally attached to our technologies. In 2011, branding consultant Martin Lindstrom set out to test our affections for, specifically, iPhones. With the iPhone 5 release right around the corner (which turned out to be the iPhone 4S, but who's counting), Lindstrom shared his findings in a *New York Times* article titled, "You Love Your iPhone. Literally." With a team of researchers, Lindstrom conducted an fMRI experiment of 16 participants aged 18 to 25 in which subjects were exposed to audio and video of a ringing or vibrating iPhone. Among other findings, he noted that the "most striking of all was the flurry of activation in the insular cortex of the brain, which is associated with feelings of love and compassion. The subjects' brains responded to the sound of their phones as they would respond to the presence or proximity of a girlfriend, boyfriend or family member." In short, we don't just really like our phones, we literally love them. We've grown up with technology and, like a family member, we love it. We are heartbroken without it.

But because these devices don't love us back or let us truly love one another, more and more people are reporting feelings of loneliness. And as we move further from a place of regular human contact (voice, touch, facial expression), our desire to connect with others will continue to grow. Thus, perhaps, the motivation behind young office-bound workers—like Cliff, myself and the lobby inhabitants of the Ace—to drop the touchscreen and pick up a fork.

"The food movement," Michael Pollan remarks in a *New York Magazine* interview with Adam Platt, is "really a communitarian movement.

What's driving people to food in many, many places is the kind of experience you can have at a farmers market. It's really a new public square."

"People," Pollan says, "have found that food gives them a lot, it gives them things that they aren't getting elsewhere in their lives."

"Food brings people together" is an old adage, mostly because it's true. Lindstrom suggests shutting off your phone, ordering a good bottle of Champagne and finding "love and compassion the old-fashioned way." Sherry Turkle says we should make space for conversation, beginning at the kitchen and dining room tables. Eating together is the single most obvious way to break our isolating habits.

Perhaps this is one reason young Americans are dining out in droves. They want to get out of their computer-induced comas and find home, or at least, interact with other humans. They want to see people, hug people, and break bread. They want something concrete to engage with after a day of participating in a virtual reality.

Chapter 2
Shut It Down

"It wasn't until I won *Top Chef Masters* that I became uncomfortable walking down Michigan Avenue by myself, because people were constantly stopping me," the revered and iconic chef Rick Bayless admitted to me over the phone, from his office in Chicago.

"It was remarkable to me," he said with excitement, "because I've been in this business for a long time. I've had a major presence on public television, I've written eight cookbooks, but it wasn't until I won *Top Chef Masters* that everything exploded."

I had asked him when he first felt famous. Bayless is a James Beard Foundation Outstanding Restaurant Award recipient for his Chicago restaurant Frontera Grill. His cookbooks have earned him the honors of Julia Child IACP Cookbook of the Year and James Beard Best International Cookbook of the Year awards. His PBS series, *Mexico—One Plate at a Time*, is in its ninth season. Bayless was—and still is—king of gourmet Mexican cooking in the U.S. One could argue that Bayless is a founding father of modern American cuisine.

Yet with all his successes, he readily admits that winning a *Bravo* cooking competition is one of the most transformative experiences in his career. The exposure has garnered him global fans, even if they've never eaten his food. Being a chef, after all, is the new version of being a rock star.

Years before my interview with Bayless, back during my time in D.C, I began to flex my cooking skills. On lazy evenings, my persistent anxieties about my life's vastly unclear trajectory would calm as I methodically chopped, stirred or baked a dinner. I learned the basics of home cooking from Ina Garten's perfectly manicured hands on *Barefoot Contessa* and Mark Bittman's quirky "Minimalist" videos: how to chiffonade herbs, roast a chicken, steam fish. I began to experiment. I made a version of my mother's chili, asked her for the secrets to the perfect latke and matzo ball, simmered tagines with lamb and chickpeas and apricots that melded full flavors, and reveled in the satisfaction of those I fed.

With food on my mind, I registered for a weekend event: Les Dames d'Escoffier's Salute to Women in Gastronomy. For $95 I could attend a full day of classes that ran the gamut of topics, from food writing to sushi rolling. The $95 price tag was my food budget for the week. But the allure of meeting Carla Hall from *Top Chef* was too much.

At eight o'clock on a Saturday morning, I drove a half hour to the Universities at Shady Grove in Rockville, Maryland. I picked up my badge and settled in the auditorium. And there she was: Carla Hall. My stomach churned with nerves. A food star was *right* in front of me. It took everything inside of me not to yell out "hootie-hoo!" and wave.

In short, I was reacting to Carla—a woman who bakes for a living—the way I had reacted to 'N Sync as a 14-year-old.

Many chefs are no longer obscured cooks—they're celebrities. They write books, host television shows, design apps and cookware lines and make game show guest appearances. We get to know, dare I say stalk, these food icons—we eat at their restaurants, read about their latest culinary ventures and watch them on TV. We follow them on Twitter by the millions.[xii]

We even read their memoirs. BaoHaus chef Eddie Huang had one of the best selling books of 2013, *Fresh Off the Boat*. Ten years ago a publisher would have scoffed at the thought of printing the life story of a 20-something, rap-loving Asian American who cooks.

Back in 1999, the Associated Press reported on "Emeril Lagasse, a gourmet master chef with blue-collar appeal who has turned the Food Network into 'Must See TV.'"

"People lined up at 6 a.m. to get seats-on a Saturday morning," the AP wrote. "Inside, the 2,000-person crowd jumped to its feet, cheering and clapping in unison as the music keyed up and an announcer shouted, 'Let's get ready to rumble.'..."

Back then, the nascent interest in all things food was, well, news. Today, multiple food-focused television networks pull in millions of viewers on a daily basis. *Hell's Kitchen*, a Fox hit starring often-incensed chef Gordon Ramsey, averaged 4.82 million viewers per episode in the 2014 season.

The last decade has encapsulated a food media explosion. Television is suddenly home to meal ideas and recipe instructions—how to toss your orecchiette or brûlée your custard. But food programs have progressed from Julia Child-esque demonstrations to competitions that steal a page from Japanese gameshows. Cooks are challenged to work with wacky ingredients like fish zygotes, sea beans and eel, while forced to kitchen MacGyver a stove from tinfoil and a hotplate, while wearing colonial garb at Gettysburg. On Bravo, you can watch *Top Chef* contestants accusing one another of being villains who overcook their teammates' halibut. Flip to the Food Network, where Guy Fieri challenges cooks to run around a supermarket. Not your thing? I can't blame you. Switch to TLC to watch a show about an Italian family piping roses on cakes, or Cooking Channel to see a cute twenty-something roam family-owned eateries across the U.S. Esquire Network has your fill for those intrigued by brewing or distilling. You can watch shows about strange foods, international foods, the history of food, cake decorating and food contests.

And now the rising generation after the Millennials—Gen Z?—is getting in on the fun with special editions of these shows, just for children: *Rachael vs. Guy Kids Cookoff* on Food Network, *Hey Kids, Let's Cook!* on PBS and *MasterChef Juniors* on Fox, featuring kids between the ages of 8 and 13, a sign that this food craze will continue to rise as the even younger generation embraces it.

And, of course, food media isn't simply TV. It's online: on blogs, social media sites, apps. You can download recipe apps that make grocery shopping a cinch. You can even record a one-minute restaurant review with your iPhone or compile a custom cookbook with a few clicks. It's now easier than ever to become obsessed.

Hand Me the Apron

After a long day in the office, working as a Business Analyst at a medical consulting group, Cate Knuff stands before a pile of raw chicken legs, carrots that need peeling, avocados to slice and sauces to be simmered. She changes from her business savvy gray dress to shorts and a t-shirt, opens her April Bloomfield cookbook, pours herself a glass of wine from the bottle left behind after a party, and begins to cook.

Cate cried when *Gourmet* magazine went under. In college, she created an independent study on the history of food in the United States. She traveled an hour and a half to see David Kessler, former FDA commissioner, speak at Princeton. She "almost peed [her] pants" when she was invited to a dinner with her "personal hero" Ruth Reichl, each of whose books, she says, she has read twice. She cooks almost every night.

"After sitting at a computer all day, I find it very relaxing to go and do something with my hands," Cate shares over dinner. "I will seek out recipes that are more involved so they'll take longer." She tells me about constructing a French Opera cake, compiled of thin layers and three different sauces: coffee, espresso and chocolate. When it was ready, she refused to let her father try it. She was bringing it to work for her coworkers.

According to a 2008 report by Mintel, an interest in cooking for those aged 18-to-24 "has been rising slowly but steadily at the same time that the proportion of those stating they prefer easy-to-prepare foods or 'rarely sit down to a meal together at home' has declined." Millennials are leaving the packaged goods in the freezer and throwing together a stir-fry or roasting a chicken instead. In February of 2011, Google launched a recipe search feature in response to the one billion recipe queries they began receiving each month. Search for "quick kale salad," get 1,560,000 results.

The Boston Center for Adult Education has noted that the faces in their cooking classes "have been getting younger and younger." Brehon Garcia-Dale, manager of the food and wine program, noted to *Christian Science Monitor* that most of her instructors are now in their 20s as well.

But Cate is largely self-taught. She learned to cook by reading cookbooks (sometimes in bed). I'm lucky enough to be her friend, as I benefit from her kitchen-dedicated hours after work. Each time I visit her, there is another beautiful meal to indulge in: mussels with a butter and garlic sauce, adobo chicken, grilled steak with a coffee spice crust. After a day at work, she wants to try her hand at something more like homemade blueberry crumble than Twitch (a video platform, for all you non-gamers).

One study notes that 65 percent of the Millennial population is "Casual Cooking Enthusiasts," compared to 53 percent of the general population. Cooking has become a "pleasurable hobby," with cooks devoting themselves to creating "elaborate" or "gourmet" meals nearly 10 times a year. "As they grow older and start families, the Mintel data suggests many Millennials will become 'Serious Cooking Enthusiasts'," summarizes the website *Millennial Marketing*. "Serious cooking enthusiasts are 16% of the overall population, but 18% of those 25-34 years old."

"When we opened our restaurant, it was not a cool thing to be a chef," Bayless said of Frontera Grill, launched in 1987. "Chefs' names would not be on restaurant menus. When I'd introduce myself, I would say, 'I'm a chef and restaurateur,' because it was okay to be a restaurateur; it was not okay to be a chef. It was super blue collar. Now, I can't tell you how many people come into our restaurant," he said, "who are 10 or 12 years old, who want to meet me and want to tell me that they want to be a chef when they grow up. That's the best thing in the world they can think of being."

"All of the sudden," Bayless said of The Food Network's influence, "food has become a sport, which makes the audience much broader and engages a lot of young men."

I think he's right. Part of the reason the number of Millennial cooks is so high is that cooking is no longer just considered a lady's home-ec course; it's a general hobby. Gone are the days when men only knew how to grill. Most celebrity chefs are (and always have been) male, and as these icons record television shows and publish cookbooks, young men are beginning to pay attention—especially when chefs are thrown into Kitchen Stadium in head-to-head battles to blend, broil and bake against the clock.

In college, my friend Dan would watch Rachael Ray on the treadmill at the gym and then try his hand at whatever she had been making that night. He found it helped him woo women. He also thoroughly enjoyed the process, proud of his penne with vodka sauce. Today, young people of both sexes are attending cooking classes and consider their kitchens a key part of the home. Partly, I believe, this is because Millennials are not just cooking for substance or to impress the Tupperware club, but to fulfill a need unmet by our technology-infused lives.

Slice, Singe, Sear, Simmer

Cooking excites each of our senses: something to chop, sniff, snap, slurp. A study conducted by JWT Intelligence found that "consumers—who now chat online with friends, tour museums virtually and play sports with the flick of a remote—feel disconnected from the tactile, 'in the flesh' world." Their survey of over a thousand adults in the U.S. and U.K. found that "the constantly connected Millennials are especially apt to feel this way. More than 7 in 10 say they increasingly crave experiences that stimulate their senses, and more than half feel increasingly disconnected from the physical world." In 2012, they predicted a top ten trend of 2013 would be "sensory explosion."

The sensory experience of eating is often underestimated. Food developer Barb Stuckey says when blindfolded, the human ear is able to detect the difference between hot water and cold water being poured. Food is so much more than taste. If our eyes and fingertips are the only senses stimulated by a computer from nine to five, time in the kitchen seems to be one antidote.

This is, of course, not just true of food. Millennials are turning to hands-on occupations as furniture builders and artisan soap makers; even blue-collar jobs like plumbing are finding a new level of interest, both due to the dismal economic situation and because of a genuine desire to fix and build and create something with real world ramifications.

"There's a sort of unrealness to the digital age we live in," Nate Pollack said to me, as we sat at the bar of his Bay Area restaurant. Nate attended UCLA, became a top-earning consultant, and when the recession came around, was laid off. His solution was to start The American Grilled Cheese Kitchen with his partner, and now wife, Heidi Gibson. "Everyone's like 'Oh, I kind of wish I was a carpenter,' or like, 'I want to do glass blowing.' People really want to create physical, tangible things.

"There's this lionization and romance of like, 'Maybe I should just be a farmer.' My friends now go on Zen retreats and work at Buddhist temples in the fields during harvest. In many ways," Nate continued, brushing his blond hair away from his eyes, "food is the most accessible, real thing a lot of us have."

Personally, coming home to a chopping block and a pile of multicolor vegetables is one of my favorite moments of the day. The elements are all laid out for me to create whatever I feel like. My laptop is closed, my phone is in the other room, along with the TV. All I have is my thoughts and the kitchen tools to help me craft the most delicious thing I can manage with the ingredients on hand. You can call or text or Gchat me, but I won't be there. I'll be in the serenity of dinnertime. Moments like these are fleeting.

Yet we can't all spend our 40-hour workweek pruning a Zen garden and for most, the seduction of technology is too potent. And here, we arrive at food porn.

It's everywhere—social media, television commercials, magazine covers. Shimmering cheddar cheese oozes from between two slices of mellow browned toast; thin ribbons of jamón Serrano have you imagining they feel like a silk dress on your tongue; foam topped beers coax you into thinking about them pressed against your perspiring neck.

You've seen it, and likely you've Tweeted or Facebooked or Pinned or Instagrammed some sultry image of food. Just admit it. 11 million posts are tagged with the word #food on Instagram. You've probably posted one of them.

But have you wondered why food porn is so enticing? Why you bother watching Mario Batali cook up a lobster fra diavolo you'll never taste?

Researchers have found that simply seeing food lights up the reward center of our brains. In fact, images of high fat foods results in "significantly greater activation" of reward centers than images of low fat foods, according to researchers at University of Washington School of Medicine. Seeing food porn can cause us to overeat and increases levels of the hunger hormone ghrelin, even when we're full. The brain's reactions give all new meaning to those close-up, dripping, glistening shots.

According to a study out of the University of Minnesota, food and drink was the number one category of interest for both men and women on Pinterest during 2012,[xiii] and food posts had the highest rate of re-pins over all other categories, including style, home and technology. Food is the single fastest growing category on Pinterest.

We really like looking at pictures of food.

"Zooming in on food makes you feel as though you're having an intimate experience with it," comments Deirdre Barrett, Ph.D., author of *Supernormal Stimuli*, in *Women's Health Magazine.*

Even reading food words are stimulating. In a recent study, researchers from Princeton University and the Free University of Berlin discovered that taste-related words—like "sweet" and "bitter"—engage the emotional centers of the brain more than literal words with the same meaning.

In the study, participants read two versions of sentences, some which included common taste metaphors and others with a literal synonym. For example, "She looked at him sweetly" became "She looked at him kindly." Meanwhile, the researchers recorded participants' brain activity. They found that sentences containing taste-related words activated areas of the brain associated with emotional processing, such as the amygdala, as well as the gustatory cortex, which allows the physical act of tasting. Pretty neat, right?

Hundreds of articles and studies have been conducted on technology's effects on child development, attention, memory skills, impulse control, sleeping patterns and more. But no one seems to be looking at the side effects of our shifting hobbies. If I were to put money on anything, I say this generation is, without a doubt, lacking in sensory stimulation, and we're finding a remedy in food.

"I think it's interesting," Michael Pollan observes in the *New York Magazine* interview with Adam Platt, "that this strikingly powerful interest in all things having to do with food coincides with a progressively more mediated, digitized life. We spend our time in front of screens. We don't exercise our other senses very much. And food is this complete sensory experience. It engages all five senses. It's a sensual pleasure." Amen, Pollan. Amen.

Households under 30 spend 75 percent more than the average household on food at home and 84 percent more on food away from home. We're investing in our time away from the computer, off our phones, far from a television, and working to build in as much of this detox time as possible.

Bite Club

I left D.C. in 2011 to backpack around Southeast Asia before starting my graduate program. I spent nearly three months wandering Thailand, Cambodia and other regions by myself, teaching English and eating dishes like gamey water buffalo *laap*, crisp piles of *bahn xeo* and peanut slathered *gado gado*. Then, I moved to New York where I started my Masters program in writing and began my research on Generation Yum.

In New York, I was forced to reconcile my new life—the lack of my backpack and the excitement of not knowing what would happen next. I was becoming accustomed to my new surroundings, and more than anything, the food culture. Streets buzzed with New Yorkers raving about their latest meals. Neighborhoods took on personalities that shifted at every corner, the scents winding from fried dumplings to pizza slices covered with melted cheese to sun festered trash.

What I quickly confronted was the ubiquitous obsession with food. While D.C. and Asia had, yes, been food-centric experiences, New York encapsulates Gen Yum culture on crack: the money spent, the time researched, the business lunches held over a pile of Belgian mussels and fries.

Within a few months, my curiosities around Millennials and food culture had reached a tipping point. I was no longer satisfied to sit back and observe. I wanted to engage and investigate. So I immediately turned to the place that the foodiest of foodies were talking about: dinner clubs.

A trend first started in Cuba, the underground restaurant, also known as "supper clubs," "closed door restaurants," "*paladares*" or "anti-restaurants," are the pinnacle foodie experience. Professional and amateur cooks alike welcome diners to a secret location for a gourmet evening. These establishments are not legally approved to serve food or alcohol. They are not registered as official businesses. They are simply places for people to gather in an exclusive, often intimate environment. They embody all I'd been thinking about: my generation's desire for intimacy, connection, new experiences and sensory excitement. I just had to find one to attend.

After some hush-hush recommendations, I discovered Bite Club, run by two novice cooks both in their early 30s (who asked that they remain anonymous). By day, one worked for a stuffed animal manufacturer, while the other was a recent transplant to the gourmet food buyers business. Several times a year, the duo would open their home to 30 visitors for a seven-course meal. Though neither had any formal training in food preparation or hospitality, they made the meal themselves and hired servers and hosts to keep the production running smoothly.

At the time, Bite Club's mailing list had grown to 6,000 people, and their events often filled to capacity within 45 minutes of the registration list's opening. I added my name to their notification list and one afternoon an email from Bite Club arrived in my inbox. In stark black and white design it encouraged me to join in "a multi-course tasting menu of pure fabulousness," and specifically outlined that, "50% of your party's required donation," of $100 per person—not including booze—was "to be paid **immediately**." The location, it said, would be revealed a few days prior to the event, along with the night's menu. My curiosity was piqued. I waved off the price tag—much like I had for my Carla Hall experience—thinking of the meal and the interesting people I hoped to meet, and signed up.

The address was sent out a few days prior to the event. It led me to a nondescript brownstone in a chi-chi Brooklyn neighborhood. A young woman dressed in black greeted me, clipboard in hand, ready to check off my name and lead me to my assigned seat in the dim-lit, crown molded living room where the hosts had arranged long tables. The space opened directly into an expansive, open-concept kitchen where diners could watch the cooking take place. I was seated at the end of a 10-person table. Sitting closest to me was a group of four women in their early-to-mid 30s, displaying large jewelry, top-end handbags and eight bottles of wine that they had brought along.

Down the table were two recent college grads, Anne and Lauren. Anne worked in financial advertising for a fabric softener company. Lauren was a veteran Bite Club diner, having traveled to Bite Club from her college in Connecticut several times in the past few years, all in the name of a good meal. She casually mentioned dining at El Bulli outside of Barcelona. She confessed to spending 90 percent of her food budget eating out. I learned that she had plans to attend a culinary management and baking program in Williamsburg, Brooklyn before opening her own bakery. When I ran into her a year later, she was tending bar at an upscale Lower East Side haunt.

Lauren said she likes showing people new things. Tonight, she had dragged Anne along to share Bite Club.

"What's your favorite bar?" Lauren asked me, eagerly awaiting my reply. I told her I was new in town. She seemed disappointed that I didn't have a hip speakeasy to recommend.

Eventually, dinner was served, beginning with an elegant, small portion of bluefish ceviche with paprika ceci, cream, horseradish and lime. The older women reached for their phones as the plates settled onto the white tablecloth. After snapping images of each dish, they pushed the food around on their plates and took small bites paired with large gulps of wine. Everyone around the table gave their evaluations: mostly positive, but I heard a whisper of, "Not enough acid." We're all judges in the age of *Top Chef.*

Next, a cold soup of watermelon with Champagne, mint, Serrano ham and feta cream. Then, a salad of tomato, burrata and grilled peaches topped with basil. I was pleased but, to be honest, not impressed. I could have made it—and probably so could you—rather easily.

"You're not finishing the burrata?" one woman exclaimed at me accusatorily, holding her fork up to nab the few last bites.

Later, another guest pulled out her phone to show me photos of every meal she had eaten in the last few years. "I don't know why I do this," she confessed, but there was evident joy and satisfaction on her face as she scrolled through the many moments of gustatory bliss.

We talked restaurants. She told me about hidden culinary gems in the Flushing Mall that I *had* to try, but her enthusiasm quickly gave way when I confessed I'd never been to Momofuku Noodle Bar, a David Chang eatery.

She tilted her head, eyebrows raised, and gave me a pitying smile. It was like she had just discovered I was of a lower caste.

Potato and parsnip gnocchi with lobster meat and caramelized shallots emerged from the kitchen and the diners again held their phones high. Then came a sad plate of under-seasoned, charred flank steak paired with a scoop of guacamole. I watched the hosts bake and flambé and roast in the kitchen, one host's shirt soaked through with sweat as he maneuvered around the kitchen before lining up each dish on the countertop for servers to fan out to waiting guests.

After the palate cleansing grapefruit granita, the final dish, molten chocolate cake, was served. I looked around the room at the many 20-and 30-somethings crowded into the Brooklyn living room. I began to wonder what we were all doing there. I, an unemployed graduate student, two barely employed recent college grads and a group of snarky *Real Housewife* wannabes, along with five other tables of young, perky urbanites who had just paid $100 each for a sub-par meal.

I left mildly hungry but full of questions: Why were broke Gen Yummers paying to eat—illegally—at an untrained stranger's house in a city full of amazing food, served in restaurants that are up to the health code, no less? Why was everyone so invested in taking pictures of their food, seemingly enjoying it more than the meal itself? I understood the connection and stimulation that food brings us, but why, I wondered, were we telling the whole world about it?

Chapter 3
Don't Eat That Yet, I Have to Take a Picture

"What's for dinner tonight?" he wrote me.

It was the first question he asked. We'd met online and within two days had discussed our favorite restaurants in New York and engaged in a flirtatious exchange on the versatility of cauliflower. Our romance blossomed over words like "lotus root," "pork belly" and "fried oysters."

A few months into my time in New York I had to face my utter bewilderment in not only how to find, but also how to define, the right partner for me. As my friends paired off, I sat before a list of profiles, unsure who to click and who to pass on.

A newbie to the online dating world, I decided to play the field: an amuse-bouche tasting of New York singles. There was the investment banker—charming, witty, but ultimately too focused on the bottom line; the doctor with an intriguing past but persistent awkward stare; and the ad guy who was too saccharine to take seriously. I was growing tired of the nerve rattling anticipation of each date and the depleting disappointment thereafter.

Then, after months of scanning profiles and exchanging disheartening messages with men I never hoped to meet, I quickly developed a charming gourmet banter with a guy who appeared to be, at least in his carefully selected profile photo, quite handsome. He had recently left his finance job to complete a year in culinary school. Swoon. For our first date, he promised to take me to a hidden restaurant on a small street. Double swoon.

Repeatedly clicking on his photos, I could see he was of medium build with a wide smile that made his eyes squint slightly on his round face. I could imagine myself with him.

Still, I decided to test this man before agreeing to meet in person. I picked one of his favorite restaurants and took myself to dinner. The food was great. A piping bowl of Thai noodle soup seeped in palm sugar, soy sauce and coriander propelled me to the stalls lining the streets of Bangkok. I groaned in satisfaction as I placed my face deep in the bowl, steaming myself in the aromas of fish sauce and simmered chicken broth. I hoped no one was looking. How could they know that I was not just celebrating a find authentic Thai cuisine in Manhattan, but a man with sagacious taste?

I decided to give Mr. Culinary a shot. On a cool winter evening, I met him at a bar on the Lower East Side. Before I left my apartment I downed a glass of wine to still my nerves and warned myself to keep my expectations in check. But he greeted me with a smile even brighter and more endearing in person. Over four glasses of Malbec, flatbread with butternut squash and shrimp and grits, I got to know him. He ordered my wine and watched for when my glass neared empty, asked if I wanted the last bite on the plate and, later, how soon he could see me again.

For our second date he sent me five options for brunch, listing each restaurant's specialty dish. We wandered his neighborhood and he pointed out his favorite cheese shop. In the days that followed, we texted one another photos of our meals apart: half-conquered pastrami sandwiches at Katz's deli, a tower of seafood at Balthazar, the various stages of a Christmas seafood pasta he was preparing for his family, my depressing bowl of stir-fry eaten on my lonely, Jewish, singleton couch. He gave me a liter of extra virgin olive oil for Christmas that he assured me was pressed in the hillsides of Italy just that week. *He understands me*, I thought.

I was thrilled to find a man with wall art listing the ingredients in a Twinkie, one who could teach me about the top producers of mascarpone and provide insight on the best homemade pasta in the city.

But after a few more dates, it became clear that that was where the seduction ended. I couldn't find more to talk about than food. And food, it seems, had blinded me from the other blaring deficiencies: religious connection, sexual chemistry, common sense of humor…you know, important stuff.

I realize now that instead of utilizing the algorithms of online dating sites, I'd thrown it all aside for my own rating system: food. His culinary prowess suggested other attractive qualities: education, income, mutual interests. I let food, in essence, indicate who this man was. I took his eating habits and gourmet knowledge as signifiers for other cultural and economic characteristics. At the time, I wasn't aware of these assumptions, but as my research into Generation Yum continued, my own behavior became abundantly more transparent.

"I think everyone at some point has a dead food blog," Diane Chang says to me in the back of a Brooklyn café. Diane would know—she's had three. They each begin with immense passion, many hours of recipe searching, restaurant prowling, food photography, uploads, downloads and hyperlinks. And then she gets bored. Diane has been blogging since before food memoirs and step-by-step recipe photo tutorials were hot commodities.

When Diane speaks, her cadence jumps and falls. She makes hand gestures that fly in the air; "likes" and "you know's" punctuate her sentences along with names of New York eateries and celebrity chefs, many of whom she personally knows.

Diane learned the how-tos of food while winding soft dough at Wetzel's Pretzels, heating sticky buns at Cinnabon and blending fruit at a smoothie shop. While her grandmother cooked traditional Taiwanese meals at home, Diane often preferred the fast food options down the street. As a young girl growing up in the San Gabriel Valley, she remembers family outings to Sizzler, for which she and her parents would dress in their finest attire. For her father, a button down shirt. Her mother, a skirt. Diane would wear a denim jumper her family had brought from Taiwan, decorated with the English alphabet, some letters missing. Diane describes it as "FOBy." Fresh off the boat.

These days, Diane has a running competition with her boyfriend: Who picks better restaurants? There is mocking, jabs, pats on the back when the falafel joint all the way out in Bay Ridge *is* fluffy and crunchy and tangy enough to have made the hour-long subway ride worthwhile. Diane readily admits her obsession with restaurant dining. It's a far cry from her days watching her grandmother cook, wondering why they couldn't just eat fast food takeout. Now, Diane will sit at dinner and parse a dish's ingredients and methods of preparation. Most of her friends work as chefs, sous chefs, pastry chefs, restaurant managers or servers. The other night she had visited friends who made pizza using a crust that had been left to ferment for three days. A few days before that, she had traveled 45 minutes out to Taste Good, a Malaysian restaurant in Queens. But Diane doesn't feel like this is exceptional behavior, especially compared to her friends. In fact, much of the time, Diane feels out-foodied.

Especially among young city dwellers, food has become the new marker of identity. Friends once exchanged albums and stories of recent concerts. Today we ask where you've eaten, chat about what you made for dinner and share a recipe for butter pickles. Both music and food fulfill similar needs for community and expressions of love and politics. Food is no longer just *food*; it carries a label (or five) and, with that, meaning.

Are you going to buy a local apple? Organic? From your favorite farm stand at the farmers market? The cheapest one at the supermarket, Walmart or Super Target? Or are you feeling motivated enough to pick the apple yourself?

There are many ways to look at the situation. You could pat yourself on the back for any of these apple purchases. The local apple is cutting down on greenhouse gasses and helping a local business. In fact, if you buy it directly from the farmer, you know exactly whom you're backing. The organic apple is supporting the organic industry, which is decreasing the use of pesticides that soak into our soil and may affect our food for generations to come (along with plenty of other confirmed and potential risks). The self-picked apple is the most intimate purchase. The cheapest apple lets you save a few cents or even dollars for a future need—and for most Americans, this is the only realistic option.

I often purchase organic or local foods that help alleviate my guilt over leaving a carbon footprint. If I exhaust half my paycheck on five grocery items at Whole Foods, I can boost my morale by admiring the USDA approved stamps on the produce in my bag. Other times I go for the cheap stuff, pleased to save a few cents.

As products gain auxiliary labels—fair-trade, local, 100% organic, USDA organic— what we put in our baskets holds more meaning than ever before. Shoppers can feel as though they're not only helping their bodies and satisfying their gastronomic needs but also, perhaps, contributing to the welfare of our planet, the well-being of farm-raised chickens and cows or the business of a small farmer. As food production becomes less opaque, consumers may choose where their food comes from and how it's produced and distributed.

As we are presented with so many options, eventually which apple you choose can become a comment on who you are, what you care about, what class you belong to.

Food, after all, is innately tied to economics and culture. Within our current food system this is especially true. Eating whole, unprocessed food has become a privilege. Organic produce is out of reach for most low-income families. (When Gwyneth Paltrow tried one week of living on $29 of food stamp benefits, she unwisely spent it on cilantro, lettuce and limes, leaving her with about 1,000 calories a day. Even for Paltrow that's not enough to survive. She only made it through four days.) Basic food education has become an indicator of class. Our most vibrant culinary traditions have historically emerged from disenfranchised, often immigrant communities. Today, the tables are turned as poor families are shut out of the opportunity to find whole ingredients to cook with, the necessary skills and the time to do it.

"Participating in foodie culture not only is a tremendous privilege, reliant on the possession of adequate economic and cultural capital, but also represents a kind of cultural hegemony," write professors Josee Johnston and Shyon Baumann in *Foodies: Democracy and Distinction in the Gourmet Foodscape.* Researcher and author Julie Guthman found that Community Supported Agriculture (CSA) and farmers' markets in California "disproportionately serve white and middle to upper income populations," even in racially diverse communities.

"Many Americans cannot afford a $4 or $5 daily coffee habit, or the $15 single-malt scotch chocolate bars that foodzie.com makes available," write Johnston and Bauman. "The popularity of Whole Foods Market (WFM) symbolizes this tension between democratic accessibility and high prices, as well as what some experts have dubbed a 'synergy' between gourmet food and natural food genres."

This obvious dichotomy shines a spotlight on the increasing rift between haves and have-nots in the U.S. As "elevated" teas, salads and burgers hit the market, a social divide is widening and ossifying around what you can afford to eat. While a coffee was once a coffee, today we all know differences between those in line for a $1 McDonald's versus a $4.50 Toby's Estate. In the 'haves' crowd, there are scornful discussions around obesity and those who continue to eat off the dollar menu. As wealthier Americans generally begin to eat healthier, will we develop increasing concern for those who cannot afford the same? Or will our society instead (or concurrently) shift further into a realm of culinary judgment and shame?

The culinary sphere now reflects the world of art: Certain restaurants are monuments to craftsmanship in its most classic form. Food trucks serve pop art and the avant-garde. Yet one huge area of art is missing. The most accessible forms of art, like street art—something that *anyone* can do with just a few inexpensive tools and a taste for excitement—currently has no reflection in food, with cost and exposure as major barriers. Even food trucks require a certain amount of capital to launch. Our street-side vendor culture—where all you need is a table and a burner—is nothing like that of other countries worldwide.

"The best thing that could happen to the world and food is if we got rid of the word 'foodie'," comedian Max Silvestri expresses. "Every time I hear the word, it makes my skin crawl. It divides the world into foodies and normals; and it's so condescending and diminutive, as if paying attention to what and how we eat was a novelty, not an essential component of human existence and a key part of being a responsible person on this planet. I throw this one back to Monsanto: I'll eat your gigantic tomatoes if they make anybody that says the word 'foodie' vomit immediately."

Gourmet food appreciation is one of the clearest signs of being a Yummer. Boomers, who are, on average, wealthier than their own parents, raised Millennials. Their elevated tastes and desires are reflected in their offspring. Starbucks was one of the first to show that, while Millennials may be penniless now, middle and upper class kids have tastes beyond drip coffee and access to their parents' wallets. (And, of course, those raised on Starbucks are no longer satisfied with the ubiquitous chain—now they want cafés like Blue Bottle or Stumptown.) Research by *Specialty Food Magazine* in 2005 shows that the typical specialty food shopper is beginning to skew young. Us Yummers appreciate a bitter espresso, silky olive oil and aged cheese, even if we can't really afford it.

Consumer desire for the gourmet is not just disrupting food markets as brands update their products and packaging, but also driving this new form of social currency between those who can afford the 'foodie' experience and those who can't, both inside and outside the Yummer population.

Vietnamese, Chinese or Indonesian Cassia Cinnamon? Whole, Cracked or Ground?

This division—of the food elite and non-food elite—has even begun to fissure within the Yummer population. Understanding the options in eating is a commodity. Some steer clear of factory-made loaves of bread and are adamant about composting, even in a small apartment (guilty). Many cookbooks incorporate ingredients that were once considered exotic and sites like Pinterest encourage extensive, photogenic experiments in the kitchen. Online recipes include buzzwords like "fair-trade," "free-range" and "single-sourced." You not only have to know how to use the ingredient, but also where to buy it. Hopefully you live some place where the ingredient is available and have the money to purchase it.

"Recipes have been steadily imbued with ever more elaborate procedures and specifications for the arcane ingredients," reported the *Wall Street Journal* in June 2012. "'1 teaspoon paprika, preferably sweet Spanish pimentón dulce,' '2 tablespoons granola, preferably homemade,' 'two small heads of garlic, preferably from a newly harvested crop.'"

On the recipe blog *Food52*, the instructions for "Pantry Pasta and Salad" note: "We're guessing you've got Dijon mustard, extra virgin olive oil, sugar, Maldon or another flaky sea salt, capers, lemons, linguine (or something similar), shallots, bread crumbs, canned tomatoes, chili flakes and garlic. If, for whatever reason you don't have those things—like, for example, you've never actually gone grocery shopping ever—you'll need those, too!"

In 2012, *The New York Times* published an opinion piece by essayist and critic William Deresiewicz on how food has replaced art as a popular product for consumption:

> Foodism has taken on the sociological characteristics of what used to be known... as culture. It is costly. It requires knowledge and connoisseurship.... It is a badge of membership in the higher classes.... It is a vehicle of status aspiration and competition, an ever-present occasion for snobbery, one-upmanship and social aggression. (My farmers' market has bigger, better, fresher tomatoes than yours.) Nobody cares if you know about Mozart or Leonardo anymore, but you had better be able to discuss the difference between ganache and couverture.

In Silicon Valley, techies bolster this trend further, with an interest in limited edition and vogue menu items. "I'm seeing a much higher demand for private whiskey tastings and stuff like that," Kristen Capella, general manager at a restaurant blocks from Twitter's headquarters told the *East Bay Express*. "[Customers from Twitter] know about the limited availability and are willing to pay for it." It's an exclusive food experience. Who wouldn't want in?

All this said, choosing what and where to eat has long indicated one's social standing, and certainly chatting about a restaurant opening or favorite cocktail has been the norm at middle class dinner parties at least since the 1950s. Back then, housewives trained in the school of Julia Child and began to challenge one another in the kitchen. "It wasn't about entertaining, it was about showing off culinary skills," David Kamp quotes food writer Betty Fussell in *The United States of Arugula*, "And absolutely competitive… because Julia was supplying us the tools for astonishing our friends."

"Kitchenwares," Kamp notes, "suddenly attained the status of fetish objects in certain American circles, where you just had to have a Le Creuset casserole dish and a crepe pan the size of a manhole cover."

But today the competition has moved beyond the home kitchen. Foodie one-upmanship is occurring beyond conversation, beyond our homes—it dominates our social media feeds, it's showing up on the shelves of supermarkets. Our food choices become more significant as we share them with others online. Everything from blogged recipes to Facebook posts about your farmer's market bounty are creating a social "culinary tension," as labeled by Johnston and Baumann, intensifying competition among a much larger population. Those culinary rivalries once limited to 1950s housewives are now pegged to online profiles, relevant among all genders, and supporting an all-day obsession.

Knowledge and consumption are the most powerful way to place yourself in a certain economic or social stratum. Millennials say no to chain restaurants, the antithesis to the know-what-you're-eating and have-what-you're-eating-be-special movement. (Unless you're doing it ironically, in which case, go ahead and tweet a picture of your pancakes and eggs from Denny's.)

Adventurous eating has become another badge of hipness. I joke that if anyone really wanted to make a killing, they should open a bug truck in the epicenter of hipness, Williamsburg, Brooklyn, to serve things like cricket tacos, sautéed grasshoppers and fried spiders. Talk about Instagram bait.

"A food journalist recently reported that 'foodie children' are the hot new accessory, and described overhearing parents proudly boasting that their children ate pig intestines at local Korean restaurants," write Johnston and

Baumann in *Foodies*. Young people trade stories of eating insects, brain, sweet breads, even placenta, and post photos of their experiences as "a badge of foodie honor and adventurism—hard evidence of 'ate there, cooked that,'" as NPR's Eliza Barclay defined it in the article "Poll: Are Your Friends Bombarding You With 'Food Porn'?"

The corporate food industry is responding to the call for exotic flavors with products such as Campbell's new "GoSoup" line that features flavors like Gold Lentil with Madras Curry and Gouda with Red Peppers. Lean Cuisine's Honestly Good line (under the tag "Whole chicken breasts. Whole grains.") offers up Pineapple Black Pepper Beef and Plum-Ginger Grain Crusted Fish. Rare dishes in hidden dining spots (ideally, on another continent) are the ultimate prize. Young Americans' expanding tastes are driving the food market by increasing the number of obscure ingredients available in supermarkets. They are also the viewers sustaining shows like Travel Channel's *Bizarre Foods* with Andrew Zimmern, where the host scampers the world, consuming foods like rotten shark meat in Iceland and chili oil pig brains in China.

This trend incorporates the effects of globalization with the desire to create in an individual identity. *I've eaten intestine. Have* you? We set ourselves apart by exploring cultures that the mainstream may find intimidating, too foreign. We want to discover the truest representation of global cuisine, even if the ingredients may (secretly) freak us out. Because even if the raw *hanchi hwe* squid with spicy *chojang* is rubbery, cold and the spice too pungent, at least it'll get a ton of "likes" on Facebook.

Ten years ago, this movement would have been impossible for one simple reason: technology. While the rift between low and high-income eaters was once just apparent in grocery stores or restaurants, today apps and social forums support online foodie peacocking. What you eat is a constant choice, made at least three times a day, and the moment you post information about your choices online, what was once a brief experience becomes a meaningful, infinite part of your identity.

You Are What You Eat and What You Post About Eating

Our food landscape is littered with options, from shopping at the market to perusing Yelp, and more than ever we are signifying our personalities in what and where we eat. But this form of self-expression and branding is just one piece of an ever-more-complicated 'Who Am I?' puzzle for Millennials.

We choose smartphone covers, create custom ringtones and set wallpaper photos of our dog or favorite celebrity. We are constantly curating: This photo or that photo? Mayfair or Kelvin? To link or not to link? In a move once saved for multinational corporations, we are branding ourselves. We are extremely self-aware, always concerned with putting the right image forward. We are obsessively, anxiously connected and dependent on the opinions of others.

Eating, like sex and sleep, is an essential human behavior. Unlike generations past, each meal can now be "shared" with hundreds, if not thousands, of people. And every time we post a snapshot of a burger we are about to devour, those food experiences gain in value in the digital currency of "platform" and "presence" and "brand." You are no longer the only one judging what and where and why you eat. So is everyone else (or, at least, that is our perception).

Young people average about 50 text messages per day, making this generation more connected to each others' thoughts, plans and decisions than ever before. We tweet, click, swipe and chat while driving, taking a bathroom break, even during religious services. Our devices are not luxuries—they're appendages.

This requires consistent upkeep of our digital and in-person identities. The way we interact with food allows us to curate both selves at once: Go grocery shopping with your friends and snap a picture to post online for your other "friends." Yet as soon as you upload a photo of beet-dusted goat cheese lollipops at Blue Hill or post an update about the cookies emerging freshly baked from the oven, that experience becomes a commodity, something of new and unclear value. Perhaps your co-workers will see it, or a friend from high school, or an ex-girlfriend. They will know you went to a four-star restaurant or spent the afternoon whipping up gourmet dough. They will see the time and money you've spent, the effort and satisfaction put in and taken out.

In 2006, Diane started to pay attention to the culinary offerings around UCLA where she was enrolled. She followed forums like eGullet and Chowhound far before most people knew of food blogs or could have guessed that food memoirs would ever be a bestselling category.

"I remember taking my cousin and a friend to this Indian restaurant outside L.A. I was so nervous because we were driving all this way, but I really wanted to try to the place—I'd read about it online." It was Diane's first restaurant-centric journey. This was also her first test: Were user-generated restaurant reviews worth reading? Would her friends think she was lame for caring so much?

When they arrived, Diane pored over the menu filled with things she had never heard of: tikka masala, vindaloo and tandoori. They decided to try it all. With the first bite, she let out a sigh of relief. Her choice didn't suck. Her friend and cousin praised her find. *How did you know?* Diane beamed with pride. The seed was planted.

Diane started cooking. She and her roommates rented an apartment off campus so they could have their own kitchen. Something about standing over the stove, chopping and stirring and poaching felt very adult, unlike her high school days at Wetzel's Pretzels. She had never been allowed in the kitchen as a child—it was her pŏ-pó's (Mandarin for "grandmother") domain. She'd been happy to wait for the spicy tofu with fermented black beans to emerge steaming from the kitchen.

Diane purchased her first cookbook from Costco. Flipping through the pages, she found recipes of foods she had never tasted. "What the fuck is veal?" she remembers thinking when she came across veal scallopini. But the ingredients were simple enough: wine, butter, sage. She decided to make it for her roommates and boyfriend. It was a success. She moved onto butternut squash ravioli, her first experience making pasta. And then olive bread. The praise rolled in.

"I think that is why I like hosting dinners. It's a nice little pat on the shoulder when you're done," she confessed. "Funny," Diane paused and cocked her head to the side and smiled. "It's like 'liking' something on Facebook. All these social networks are so smart," she said, and I could see her thoughts forming. "They've tapped into the thing that human beings want: gratification."

Diane took her new culinary smarts online and started several blogs: one to rip on British superstar chef Jamie Oliver, another to pair music and food and the third to showcase her grandmother's recipes. Diane wants to share her discoveries with others. Beyond that, each experience feels more momentous the instant it is posted online. And that "little pat on the shoulder" and "likes" is, without a doubt, a driving force of what's made Diane an obsessive food fanatic.

"Look what I'm eating, asshole."

In June 2012, a recent college grad, Katherine Markovich, wrote a witty and snarky essay for *McSweeney's*: "An Open Letter To People Who Take Pictures of Food With Instagram." In it, she addresses a hypothetical amateur photographer:

> You posted an Instagram-ed picture of a handful of blueberries the other day. What would your day have been without those blueberries? Would you have felt a little less connected to the earth and, ultimately, yourself? Would you have felt guilty about letting all of nature's candy go to waste? Or perhaps the real question is this: how disappointed would you have felt if your beautiful, plump blueberries got less than 15 likes? It would have made blueberry picking pretty pointless, right? But no, you are popular and people like to feel earthy and spontaneous by living vicariously through you and your blueberry-picking adventure. So people leave comments like, "*Yummy. <3. Jealous!!!*" And sadly the commenter is actually jealous and thinks that you are rustic and outdoorsy and simple, but in an *old-timey Norman-Rockwell-America-is-really-great!* way. You were creative enough to think of this super-fun activity, one that does not involve being cooped up inside, or drinking, or giving into any of the other demands of capitalist America. This makes you better than all of us. And this also gives you permission to take pictures of what you made for dinner.

And then you did.

What's so brilliant about the essay is that it blatantly calls out what many of us are already aware of: We use social media to promote ourselves. While in-person mealtime is all about connection, online mealtime focuses on self-promotion. Social networking sites are a narcissist's best friend. Our egos flourish in a world of continuous (if superficial) approval from friends and family: "Great pic!" "Ooo yum," "Awesome dress!"

Jean M. Twenge, Professor of Psychology at San Diego State University, and W. Keith Campbell, Professor and Head of the Psychology Department at the University of Georgia, wrote a book titled *The Narcissism*

Epidemic: Living in the Age of Entitlement about, guess who? In it, they actually shift the blame somewhat from us, and instead, focus on Baby Boomer parents. The authors suggest that parents who buy into celebrity and looks-obsessed culture encouraged "look at me" and "self-admiration" attitudes in their offspring. Current lore says that today's parents praise their children endlessly, protect them from punishment and want to be their friends instead of the boss. Twenge and Campbell may verge on the bombastic, but a shift in parental expectations and methods indisputably occurred in much of America between the Baby Boomers' own upbringing and raising their own Gen Y children.

So the critics are right, then: We're self-obsessed! While young people have *always* had solipsistic tendencies, in the ever-expanding digital landscape Gen Y has unprecedented amounts of fuel. In fact, according to the National Institutes of Health, 58 percent more college students had a "high narcissim" scale score in 2009 than in 1982.

We are really great at showing other people just how great we are. In 2010, York University student Soraya Mehdizadeh tested 100 Facebook users, ranging in ages 18 to 25, with self-esteem and narcissistic self-reports. She analyzed self-promotional content, such as photos and status updates, on each of the participants' profiles. She concluded that the feedback Facebook users receive from others, such as likes, shares and comments, "can act as a positive regulator of narcissistic esteem." In fact, it has been found time and again that the more narcissistic you are, the more likely you are to participate in online social networking forums. The flip side is that those with low self-esteem are also more likely to be social media users, feeling the need to project a certain image of themselves and connect with peers via "likes" and comments.

When I post photos of what I've cooked or eaten (or am about to eat), I do it for three reasons: to share the experience with friends, to develop my brand as a food writer and maybe, if I'm being honest with myself, to show off. *I did this! I ate here! Look how pretty my dinner is!* It's a terrible thing to face; that my tweets about making latkes with my family are partially to say 'Happy Hanukkah' to friends and partly to say 'I had awesome latkes, boo-yah non-latke eaters.' Perhaps my moments of eating with friends and cooking is about community, but I can now admit that the time I spend promoting it online often has far less admirable motivations.

I put forth my theories about Gen Yum—our anxieties and our narcissism—to Anthony Bourdain. He had agreed to speak with me about Gen Yum right before he departed to the Congo for a taping of *Parts Unknown*, his television show on CNN. We had met a few weeks earlier at a food event. As hors devours were passed around, I sheepishly clutched a notebook and rehearsed my lines over and over in my mind as I awaited an opening in the crowd to approach him. Somehow, I caught his attention and weeks later I sat shaking in my office chair on the phone with him.

"I was talking with a couple of friends about this generation of young diners," Bourdain said right off the bat. "These guys have rather famously and humorously been complaining about all these hipsters coming to their restaurant and taking pictures of all the food and all the rest, and I finally said, 'Look, lets face it. All these people you're calling hipsters are what's called 'young people,' you old fuck,'" he laughed, "'and you're benefitting mutually from it.'"

"Absolutely the engine of dining, even fine dining now, across the board, is this generation of seemingly food obsessed people who are willing to drive an hour and a half for a sweet taco or save up money—that my generation would have spent on cocaine—to go to Le Bernardin," Bourdain confidently stated.

"At every level of dining you're seeing either new businesses reacting to that or responding to this new interest, taking into account the changing demographic in their dining rooms. Because it's at every level. It's not just people looking for the ultimate authentic *tom yam* soup or Chinese tripe dish that they heard about at some mall out in Flushing," he said, referring to the largely Chinese area of Queens, New York, "it's people who are actually saving money to go to places like Le Bernardin, people who cannot afford to eat in those restaurants."

I was relieved. He stole the words right out of my notebook. Generation Yum is indeed an anomaly, and the impact of this anomaly is being felt in a variety of ways.

"My generation, we defined ourselves by the record we carried under our arm," he said to me of his Baby Boomer cohort. "That spoke for us: If you walked around with a Stooges album under your arm or Cream, that's who you were.

"A powerful signifier as well was what drug you did and the users of that drug you then associated with. That's where you spent your money. The recreational ideal was to have enough money to spend on cocaine," he remarked, recalling his days of young adulthood in the 70s and early 80s. "I think for whatever reason the real tectonic shift has been that young people today are spending their disposable income on food."

And those food choices, I countered, are then plastered online for all to see, acting as the new form of identification.

If you want to follow anyone on social media, you should follow Tony. His posts are insightful, funny and often times, drool-worthy (that is, except when he posts photos of his Jiu-Jitsu training). His Instagram captures snapshots of pillowy, bright orange sea urchin and international beer bottles cradled on the beach, mixed with snippets of sincere reflections along his travels.

His following is immense: nearly 600,000 followers on Instagram and over 2 million followers on Twitter. If anyone is to have thoughts about the ethics of tweeting—and specifically food postings—it's likely to be him.

"I understand very much that when I tweet, '*The Taste*, new time 9pm tomorrow,' that's business," he said. (*The Taste* is a blind-tasting television show where he serves as a judge.) "I also understand that I pay a price for doing that," he honestly stated, in true Bourdain fashion. "I'm really very wary of using social media as a marketing tool because obviously, I bleed out a little bit every time I do that. I really try to keep that at a minimum.

"On the other hand," he confessed, "I am a passionate—in spite of my snark to the contrary—I am a passionate tweeter of pictures of food."

I asked him about the narcissism factor, the need-for-approval factor.

"Sometimes I wonder whether it's an aggressive act. Sometimes it is. You're not being sincere. You're not 'sharing,'" he said, mocking the idea of benevolent social media posts. "You're rubbing people's nose in it. You're saying, 'Look. Look what I'm eating, asshole. You're eating Cap'n Crunch with skim milk. I'm eating some wild hare with truffles, yo.' It's mean."

"Rather than the thing itself, the representation of it becomes more pleasurable, has more of a thrill to it, more of a punch," says Greil Marcus, famed writer and Chez Panisse investor, of our current obsession with food and sharing. "It's like people who film themselves having sex and like to watch the monitor while they're having sex."

While many of us consider mealtime a hands-on relief from our social media-infused lives, we also use food experiences as a means to enhance our online selves: blogging, texting, Instagramming and hoping others will "like" our creations. If what we're seeking with our food preoccupation is emotional connection and a break from the virtual *in the moment*, why are we so obsessed with documenting it all?

Marcus has, in many ways, been the God of hipness since the '70s when he was the music reporter at *Rolling Stone*. With naturally slicked back silver hair and round glasses, he still exudes a cool vibe. Back in his *Rolling Stone* days he befriended Alice Waters, now widely regarded as the creator of the local and organic food movement with her world-famous restaurant, Chez Panisse. Decades ago, over dinner in Berkeley, California, Greil encouraged Alice to open a restaurant. Since that fateful conversation, Greil has watched Chez Panisse's clientele and menu evolve. When Marcus recently saw a woman filming her meal there, he was "dumbfounded."

"I assume," Greil pondered during an afternoon chat in his office, "that this is narcissism run amok; that people want other people to know what they're eating in real time. And it strikes me as utterly bizarre."

Do we post that "Instagram-ed picture of a handful of blueberries" to spread the joy of eating beautiful blueberries with friends or to brand ourselves as earth-loving hippies? Perhaps Markovich is on point when she asks in her essay: "How disappointed would you have felt if your beautiful, plump blueberries got less than 15 likes?"

Us Yummers are so intrigued by food, in fact, that we can manage to hit pause at mealtime to take a picture, set a filter and post it *before* eating—performance overtaking instinct.

We actively and constantly pursue validation from our peers. Like my profile photo? My haircut? Narcissists *and* people with low self-esteem are most likely to use social networking sites. We present ourselves as thoughtful, well-rounded, popular, cultured—or edgy, hardcore, blasé, depending on who is looking. We are different on LinkedIn and Facebook and OkCupid. Online, researchers note, we can be our "hoped-for selves," our ideal characteristics uploaded from Photoshop. Validation also means competition. You are judged. And more and more often, you are judged by what you eat as we continue to use food as the new identifier, the new album carried under the arm.[xiv]

So it this all bad? I asked Bourdain.

"Whether or not you enjoy taking pictures of food, or whether your find it weird or distracting is besides the point," Bourdain countered. "The whole notion of submissively submerging yourself in a food and wine experience—that at the end of the day is good. Not just for you as a chef or as a business person," he said, referring to his chef friends who find annoyance in the constant tableside iPhone clicks, "but probably on balance, good for the world.

"What else do you want young people to be interested in right now? Should they be taking shots of celebrities? Should they be taking pictures of pro football players? Of sports memorabilia? Of cars? What better than something as interesting, ever-changing, and central to culture, and sensuality, than food?"

Though we may be imposing some forms of judgment and elitist behavior through our food obsession, at the same time, Bourdain argues, we as a generation are also becoming involved in one of the most human topics. An interest in food is an interest in food. So what if someone feels the need to tell everyone they went to Brooklyn Fare and ate a $200 meal? Either way, we'd likely find a way to judge each other on something. And maybe, just maybe, with a growing interest in kale chips, we'll eventually pay attention to the more important side of things, like food inequality, farm subsidies and so on. In the land of social media, our desire for validation and brand performance would be taking place with or without the simmering bowls of pho. And to Twenge's point, even without social media, we'd likely be displaying our better-than-you mindset in some way, as a result of our Boomer-doting upbringing.

Perhaps the Instagramming of food and social judgment of food is a tangential offshoot of an entirely unrelated characteristic of this generation. While we have a craving for community on one end, we're also obsessive over self-branding and newsfeeds. And Bourdain's comment is quite valid. The real takeaway here is: We're starting to care and learn about food.

A brief stint at *Bon Appétit* educated Diane on the details of recipes: "Like, what's ras el hanout? What is that spice blend? Why is it thirteen different spices?" she asks, noting that her time at the food magazine helped expand her focus from restaurant dining and dinner parties to actually start looking at the ingredients that made up the food she was consuming and cooking.

Diane launched a new blog at the start of 2013, titled *Eating Pŏ-Pó's*, homage to her grandmother. It's part recipe building for a potential cookbook and part inspiration for a pop-up restaurant. Lately, she spends evenings on the phone with her grandmother, who will tell her to add a dash of this, a pinch of that. No measurements, though; Pǒ-pó can't help her there.

In the spring of 2013, Diane held a one-night pop-up restaurant at a bar in East Williamsburg, Brooklyn, where she served a dish she titled pǒ-pó, a mashup of her grandmother's recipes for scallion pancakes and braised beef shank, to make the ultimate Chinese burrito. She and two friends squashed themselves into the far back corner of the small, wood paneled bar. They unfolded, scooped, wrapped and plated over 90 orders of beef and vegetarian pǒ-pó. She had spent a month testing eight variations of the dish, inviting friends over to critique and provide suggestions. The day before the event, she and her boyfriend stayed up until 2am, crafting 120 scallion pancakes from scratch. Her friend sliced cucumbers, as well as his finger, while creating rounds for pickling. Diane called in sick to work the next day. She toasted and ground Szechuan peppercorns. She blended her own five-spice mix.

The night of the event, she printed menus with descriptions in both English and Mandarin. She fried the pancakes and ran them out to tables. An "enduring [takeaway] from this experience was being able to share the food I grew up on with other people," Diane wrote later.

Unlike some of Diane's previous food experiences, this wasn't just about pats on the back or showing friends how awesome her grandmother's recipes are. It also gave Diane the time to unravel recipes she had only seen from the sidelines, spices she had never toasted herself, dough she had never perfected with her own hands. This time, instead of passively watching her pǒ-pó cook or eating a restaurant meal, she was the one figuring it all out.

Chapter 4

Amish Chicken Raised In Cage-Free Environment, Fed Chickpeas From Certified Organic Seeds, Grown at an Optimal Altitude and Locale For Clean Air and Rain, Served On a Compostable Plate

Giancarlo heard the snap of the captive bolt gun. Thack! Like someone clanging two pieces of metal under water. Then an immediate quake as the 1,300 pound animal hit the cold concrete floor. A shock rumbled through Giancarlo's body as he looked over his shoulder at the scene. His hands were covered in bright red blood; one hand grasped a knife while the other steadied the carcass before him, resting on a metal table. He shook with the reverberation of the animal's rapid death. Giancarlo felt an electric buzz in his spine as he replayed the moment. He wouldn't be eating his lunch that day.

It was his first day on the kill floor. A few weeks earlier he'd been at his old job in a cardiology office, checking in patients and calling insurance companies. There, he'd held a pen and clipboard. Days later, a knife and an amputated hoof. Giancarlo knew most people thought he was nuts, including his new boss. A month earlier, Giancarlo had gone on a meat processing tour of the facility with his friend James. Afterward, he asked the owner for a job. "So you're a city guy that wants to be a farmer?" The owner inquired.

"Pretty much, yeah," was Giancarlo's reply.

One of my favorite victims of the anti-Yummer backlash is the overly food conscious hipster. This is mocked in full force in one episode of *Portlandia,* a television show on IFC: specifically the scene in which two characters, Peter and Nance, barrage a soft-spoken waitress with questions about the origins of a chicken dish on the menu. As they sit with glasses of white wine before them, they learn that the chicken is a "heritage-breed, woodland-raised chicken that's been fed a diet of sheep's milk, soy and hazelnuts." But this information is not enough to appease these Portland, Oregon diners. They want to know if the chicken is local and organic, and if so, what kind of organic?

"Is that USDA organic or Oregon organic or Portland organic?" Nance asks the unflustered waitress. They want to know if the hazelnuts fed to the chickens are organic as well. And how big is the plot of land these chickens roam on? The waitress returns with a profile of the chicken.

"His name is Colin," she informs them. They wonder if he had a lot of friends and about the people who raised him. In the end, they decide to go check out the farm before placing their order.

Though *Portlandia* takes the familiar trope to ridiculous heights, it created more than a few twinges of recognition, judging by its popular reception. Yummers want to know where their food is from. We want to know how it is made, who raised it, who grew it, nurtured it. We want to know how our ingredients came to be, the details of their origins. What are they, really? And how can I learn the process?

This push for the "real" has much to do, of course, with the backlash against big agriculture and the dubious state of food in the United States. Food fraud runs the gamut from horsemeat in frozen "all beef" meals, to pork bung—that's anus, for those unacquainted—being passed off as calamari. Yum. Fast food has resulted in a wide variety of meals that our grandparents would hardly recognize.[xv] Traditional Chicken McNuggets, for example, McDonald's staple dish that was my childhood crack, are filled with modified food starch, salt, seasoning (comprised of autolyzed yeast extract, wheat starch, safflower oil, dextrose and citric acid), sodium phosphates and natural flavor (botanical source). Oh, and some chicken. Packaged goods list unpronounceable preservatives; "diet" foods can include carcinogenic substitutes and wood pulp. And industrial farms use pesticides that not only harm the human body but also the earth, for untold generations to come.[xvi] As consumers become more aware of the additives and fillers in our foods, they request more "real," honest and safe ingredients.

People have long wanted to know what goes into their food. The counterculture of the '60s promoted macrobiotic diets, whole foods, and local ingredients, but—as with experiments in communal living—they ultimately were promoted by a small population and often satirized by mainstream culture. The current enthusiasm for "local" and "simple" food is unprecedented. A 2012 consumer study by ThinkSplendid found that 80 percent of a test group, born between 1979 and 2000, wanted to know more about how food is grown. People want answers: Is this USDA organic, local, grass-fed, cage-free, pesticide-free? Was this produced in a factory or by human hands? If the latter, were those humans working in safe conditions? If the former, what multisyllabic preservatives are also being added?

Today, more restaurants list the farm where their produce comes from, or the body of water their seafood was reeled in from. Seasonal menus are in. Grocery labels are becoming more and more specific. Five Acre Farms, a brand of supermarket products in New York, attaches dainty red labels onto each of their products that read in bright, bold lettering: "Positively Local." On the flip side of the label is a photo of the farmer who milked the cow that produced your milk: Don and Seth McEachron, photographed in baseball caps and button-down shirts alongside a *Got Milk* banner. They are fourth and fifth generation farmers from Battenkill Valley, New York. "In 2010," the label says, "they won Cornell's top prize for milk. They grow all their own feed and use a mixed breed herd for higher calcium counts." Why the heck do we care?

Giancarlo has a full dark brown beard that hides most of his face. His round, blue eyes pop between the scruff and the edge of his baseball cap. His smile shows a mild gap tooth. Giancarlo received his degree in economics from the University of Colorado in 2006. He grew up in an upper-middle-class household in Colorado. His father works as a cardiologist, his mother as a massage therapist. He grew up eating Italian dinners at home and expanded his palate on family trips to New York where he became acquainted with caviar at Aureole at the age of four. He remembers the obligatory suit and tie, as well as the waiters looking on in delight as their pint-sized customer devoured the pricy delicacy. "And then I fell asleep," Giancarlo recalls, remembering the restaurant's puffy walls, which provided adequate comfort.

Later, his story took on shades of *Portlandia*. Giancarlo wanted to know where the proverbial Colin was raised so badly that he decided to become a part of that process. Today he is the one bringing Colin to your plate. Well, not Colin. In fact, not chickens. But cows and lambs and pigs.

"I wanted to know where the animals that we eat came from," Giancarlo explained. "A lot of people go to the store and they just see pieces of meat in Styrofoam with Saran Wrap over the top of it and don't really think about what goes into making it, to how that product gets there."

Efforts to deconstruct the food chain from its industrial belt are taking place on a variety of levels through the Millennial generation. In San Francisco, one way it plays out is in the competitive world of coffee. On a summer trip to the Bay area, my friend Michelle suggested we stop in a Four Barrel coffee shop. There, we were greeted by a drip coffee bar—clear jars filled with roasted beans, each labeled with their origin country and tasting notes—and a lanky, plaid-shirted, bearded young man. (I know, not very descriptive for San Francisco.) I asked him to explain drip coffee to me.

"Coffee brewing is a solubility reaction," the bubbly barista began to explain as he prepared the grounds and Chemex flask for my drip coffee order, asking first if I preferred "chocolaty" or "floral" coffees. (He described my coffee with notes of maple syrup, apricot and honey, none of which, I must admit, I was able to detect.) My coffee guru, Alex, was a Pre-Med student at Wesleyan. After graduating in 2009 he became fascinated by coffee brewing. Alex swapped a future in medicine for in-house coffee classes and tastings, also known as "cuppings."

Alex grew up drinking chai tea and did not develop a coffee habit until college. There, during his one hour break between Organic Chemistry and Physics, he would hang out in the science library, read *The New York Times* and drink "the worst latte in the world." After returning to his hometown of San Francisco on college breaks, he realized that not all coffee tasted like the scorched lattes of Wesleyan. During a semester abroad in South Africa he developed an interest in wine. When he came home, he realized, as he put it: "All this knowledge that I've developed around tasting can be attributed to other things, like coffee."

"The idea of terroir is a really romantic one," Alex elaborated as he poured and timed my brew, artfully performing the Chemex balancing act. "Agricultural products are so specific to innumerable factors that contribute to how they taste in the end. The realization that coffee was part of that story was really interesting to me." The mix of geology, climate, plant genetics, geographical impacts and mechanics drew Alex into the world of brewing.

"I do this at home," Michelle said, pointing to Alex as he slowly poured steaming water over coffee grounds, checking the weight of the flask and his timer for the best possible results.

"Do you time it and measure it?" I asked, mildly bewildered. Michelle nodded. I was already stunned to learn that she, an unemployed Amherst grad living with her mother, routinely paid $4.50 for a cup of coffee. But now I knew that she also invested in Chemex machinery and spends the time heating and slowly brewing each cup at home. Michelle and Alex both clearly thought I was missing out on something.

I began to think about what draws this generation, over others, to uncover the roots of our meals. We are calling for "real" ingredients so loudly that even one of the largest fast food chains, Chipotle, is answering by only serving naturally-raised, antibiotic free meats with mostly organic, family-farmed, local produce. Recently they announced they're going GMO-free. Panera Breads has banned the use of artificial ingredients and even Kraft, the mega-producer of processed foods, announced it's swapping out those Yellow #5 dyes for natural ingredients like turmeric and paprika in Kraft Mac N' Cheese. McDonald's has produced a number of videos on YouTube with the lead: "Our food. Your questions." One inquiry is "What's in McDonald's food?" "We're ready to tell you what you want to know about our food," says the Director of Strategic Supply, Rickette Colins. They also have a video series titled "Proud of Our Suppliers." Nothing like this happened in the '70s in response to the hippies.

So why are so many Yummers—those professionally involved in food and those Pinteresting bystanders—all demanding recognizable, organic, true ingredients? Perhaps it's one of the only areas left where we actually have any hope of gaining a full understanding of its parts. There is a comfort in knowing the details, of feeling like you're in a position of power to decide the final result. We want food that is easy to understand. There isn't much else we can do that with anymore.

Do you know how your iPhone works? Or the Internet? Or practically anything plugged into your wall? How about your now key-less car ignition? That scale that reports your body mass index and percentage body fat? Do you understand the housing crisis? The intricacies of government taxation codes, student loan systems or the stock market? It seems everything continues to get more and more complicated. Understanding a meal is a fairly effortless way to master every single element.

"It's like really rewarding; it's a constant reward loop," says 27-year-old Lola Milholland of making her own food. "The more you grow or the more you cook or the more you farm, the better it becomes. You get constant pleasure from it. And in a time in history when things feel kind of out of control or enormous, it's a really enjoyable and self-benefitting way to participate."

Perhaps this demand for basic back-the-earth foods is just one way we're attempting to subdue our ever-growing anxieties as a generation.

"Rapid change is the only constant," writes David Burstein in *Fast Future*, "and the chief survival skill for millennials is keeping our balance in this sometimes mad, sometimes surreal, always changing, topsy-turvy world."

The effects of growing up in a "topsy-turvy" environment are blatant in generational stress and anxiety levels. A 2008 stress survey conducted by Booth Research found that two-thirds of Americans ages 18-to-24 are feeling overwhelmed, a higher percentage than any other age group surveyed. A 2012 American Psychological Association (APA) survey also found that younger Americans report higher levels of stress, on average, than any other age group. Why are we overwhelmed?

To begin, unlike many of our parents whose futures were largely laid out for them by family businesses or financial limitations, us Millennials have more financial support yet entirely blank futures. According to the APA survey, over 52 percent of Millennials report having lain awake at night in the past month due to stress. We are what we do…which is what, exactly? And how are we ever going to save enough money to reach the milestones of adulthood if we can't find a job?

We travelled down the path of check marks, test scores, APs and college applications only to emerge at the other side, degree in hand, with no job market or financial guidance. The carefully orchestrated route left us, ultimately, powerless and often confused.

Unemployment is high, parental adoration even higher, yet security is low. Underemployment for young college grads hovered around 19 percent in 2012, with many taking jobs they didn't want or even, worse, unpaid internships. (Other reports put the number closer to 13 percent but are careful to note that as many as 1.7 million 18-to-29 year olds are not being counted as unemployed because they've simply given up looking.) If we are lucky enough to get hired, our lower wages mean that the wealth gap between older and younger Americans continues to widen at record speed, as median net worth of those under 35 plummets. This, of course, makes it harder for this generation to save: for housing, graduate school, kids. You know, the future.

A report by PEW Research Center titled *The Boomerang Generation* states that, of the 24 percent of adults ages 18-to-24 who are living at home due to economic difficulties, "nearly eight-in-ten say they don't currently have enough money to lead the kind of life they want, compared with 55% of their same-aged peers who aren't living with their parents." Let's break this down: Over half of those 18-to-24 who are still living on their own feel they don't have enough money. And 80 percent of those who have resorted to bunking up with mom and pop still aren't saving enough to lead the life they want (and they represent over a quarter of young adults in America)!

What makes this situation even worse is that we were so perfectly primed to think that we were in control—that we could decide how we wanted to live our lives and who we wanted to be. Jean Twenge, also the author of *Generation Me: Why Today's Young Americans Are More Confident, Assertive, Entitled--And More Miserable Than Ever Before*, says Generation Y has been taught to put themselves first. Summing up Twenge, *Psychology Today* reports:

> Reliable birth control, legalized abortion and a cultural shift toward parenthood as a choice made GenMe the most wanted generation of children in history. Television, movies and school programs have told them they were special from toddlerhood to high school and they believe with a self-confidence that is impressive. GenMe, unlike the Baby Boomers are not self-absorbed, they're self-important. They take it for granted that they're special, independent, and don't need to reflect on it.

We were raised in a world of excess. Shows like *Cribs* and *Pimp My Ride* emphasized wealth and fame. At the same time, reality shows like *The Real World*, *Big Brother* and *Survivor* showed us that a talentless ordinary Joe could easily become a celebrity. Immediate success became the goal and examples of flamboyant wealth infiltrated our TV sets. Want to be a rock star? Upload a video to YouTube. Then go buy 10 boats.

Yet our parents' confidence and assurances that we're "special"—and casting calls for reality shows—have not, in most cases, turned us into hyper-successful adults. And at a certain point, if you're jobless and broke, you'll start questioning why you're such a failure, why you can't seem to understand how to play the game right. We can't all be Justin Bieber (thankfully) or Mark Zuckerberg. If we're not famous in two seconds, if we can't achieve our goals at a record pace, what does that say about us?

This generation also faces entirely unique pressures that will likely plague all generations that follow us as well. We, unlike any generation before, have had to learn how to manage our online avatars. What we wear to school is no longer the primary concern—it's our profile photo. We must curate two identities instead of one. Research from the University of Edinburgh Business School shows stress levels skyrocketing with an increase in Facebook friends. Having one more social circle to navigate and edit and control is adding to our already frazzled existence.

There are also new dangers to take into consideration: privacy risks, rapid spreading of rumors, unwanted "friends," stalking, hacking. Suddenly the game of telephone doesn't seem so intimidating. Try a nasty, anonymous online post, or a floating sext put into the wrong hands. A survey reported by *The Atlantic* found that: "A whopping 98 percent of respondents don't fully trust the information available on [the internet]." And rightly so. And that's putting aside the unnerving notion that few of us understand how any of it really works, anyway.

While every generation faces its challenges—heck, I'm not trying to say that Yers have it worse than all others—the many small bits of anxiety are adding up into a highly unsettled group of young Americans.

It's no wonder someone like Giancarlo, pushed through the high-pressure ranks of boarding school and a family with ample expectations, began to feel a craving for simplicity; the same happened to Alex and Michelle and Diane. In a land of unending questions and very few concrete answers—muddled by new technologies, a housing crisis, sky-high unemployment rates and Edward Snowden—looking to a recipe with set instructions and clear parts and products is a welcome change. In short, we're breaking down what we can, to its most basic parts. Can we do that with our iPhones? Maybe, but it's going to take a *lot* of effort (and maybe breaking into Apple). Can we do that with the meals we eat each and every day—why, yes.

Perhaps understanding the most basic roots of our sustenance (whether breaking down a cow or reading the label on a package of rice) and experiencing a predicable result is providing a bit of serenity for this overwhelmed cohort of young Americans.

My hours of cooking on a step stool in my miniature apartment, half drunk and starving were starting to make more sense to me.

The Recipe to Life

"When I moved to New York I didn't eat fish or cheese or mushrooms or almost anything," Peter Meehan tells me over espressos at a hidden coffee joint behind a clothing store in SoHo. The highly regarded writer is in a red plaid t-shirt, hair disheveled. Many know Meehan from his four-year stint as *The New York Times* "$25 and Under" columnist, and later, author of the "Grass Fed" column. Or, his name may be familiar from the bylines of several cookbooks, or the masthead of *Lucky Peach*, which he co-founded. But before all that, and before he knew anything about food, Meehan arrived in New York City to be with his girlfriend of several years, now his wife, while she attended Parsons New School for Design. The couple met back in Oak Park, Illinois, at the age of sixteen, where Meehan grew up in an Irish-Italian Catholic family. At the time of the New York move, Meehan felt lost, directionless. He was a college dropout who "smoked a lot of grass." Without a foundation and in a new city, he began to integrate himself into his girlfriend's social circle, which happened to include several women of East Asian descent. They began to cook dinner together, during which the ingredients and methods often left Peter dumbfounded. "I had to learn to like the food that people were making," he confessed.

Food "became a puzzle to untangle." Putting his funk aside, he purchased *La Technique: An Illustrated Guide to the Fundamental Techniques of Cooking* by Jacques Pépin and realized, "Oh, if you learn these steps, you can make this food." He began unraveling the culinary conundrums.

"One night," he tells me, long before he met food writer Mark Bittman, whom he later worked for at PBS and the *Times*, "we'd just bought Mark Bittman and Jean-Georges' *Cooking at Home with a Four-Star Chef*, and we were making a slow baked salmon, which seemed like the most fucking elegant thing that ever happened in my entire life at that point, and I went to the store and I realized there was red and white wine. That thought had never occurred to me, that there were two colors of wine. And I'm like, 'Oh, fuck I gotta figure this whole thing out.' So I got super into wine." Meehan received an advanced certificate from the Wine and Spirits Education Trust. After a few years, he was an expert at food as well; his nascent knowledge of East Asian cuisine was built up. He was comfortable with Japanese food, Malaysian food. He could shop in Chinatown and was unafraid to order anything. And he knew what drinks to pair with a meal. The unnerving feeling of lacking control was gone. He had power, at the very least, over dinner.

"I feel stupid about it sometimes," Meehan says of his interest in food, "'cause now everyone's interested in it."

Meehan was a bit ahead of the curve. He started out before the food blogs, before Emeril's "BAM!" or Rachael Ray's "EVOO," a bit before technology was so thoroughly infused in our lives (current omnipresence aside, Facebook was only invented in 2004). Meehan is Gen X, not Gen Y. He was right on the cusp, feeling the undertow before the wave had fully formed. Nonetheless, his experience of unveiling the mysteries of a plate of food, working his way through cookbooks and culinary traditions, speaks directly to the Gen Yers taking up his lead.

We have returned to the kitchen in great numbers: not just young mothers reading Julia Child (though many still do), but also high schoolers and college students, childless and largely budget-minded twentysomethings.

28-year-old biomedical researcher Julia Gilden recalls her days of artisanal food making during the completion of her Ph.D. in San Francisco. After spending hours upon hours in the lab—moving small amounts of liquid from one test tube to another, logging results into the computer, researching cell biology and the behaviors of African sleeping sickness—she would return home to make semi-aged cow milk cheese or strained yogurt. She appreciates the demystification process, "that I can turn milk into cheese," understanding the craftsmanship needed to make it really good.

"The thing about science is that you can do everything right and the experiment still doesn't work…and that's just really not the case with food. The results are very predictable. You can pretty much be assured of a rewarding result." She was in control of the final product. Now, she grows her own kale, peas, snow peas, radishes, asparagus, tomato, eggplants and peppers at home.

"It's a unique thing that I am able to create, to better the way we see food, the way we eat," Giancarlo tells me as we sit in a smoothie shop in Lower Manhattan.

I went to visit Giancarlo at Dickson's Farmstand Meats in New York City. Dressed in a long white butcher coat, Giancarlo excitedly took me on a tour of the facility. Behind the storefront is a New-York-apartment-sized refrigerator stacked floor to ceiling with cuts of beef and pork, racks of sausages hanging in rows. The room smells sweet, the air crisp. Buckets of knucklebones, joints with pearly white cartilage, shine beneath bright pink remains of connective tissue. Giancarlo works with a scimitar, an Arabian sword that allows him to cut with ease. When that isn't strong enough, there's a woodchuck-like bone saw directly behind him. I shudder thinking about how easily a finger or hand or arm could be lost with one unfortunate slip. As Giancarlo trims pieces of tenderloin, he chucks the scraps into a bin behind him without even looking, and they land with impressive precision. When one of his fellow butchers mocks him in profane Spanish, Giancarlo flings the excess cuts of fat across the room.

His favorite part of the job is "breaking days," when shipments of whole animals are delivered. He and his coworkers begin at prepare at 8am for the one cow, eight to nine pigs and five lambs on their way. Giancarlo will change the trays of meat in the counter case, remove soiled paper that is turning an unappetizing deep purplish brown, then unroll and cut new pieces of parchment. When the trucks arrive, there's a rush. Giancarlo attaches his weight belt and jacket and runs to the loading dock. They have to transfer and break down the animals as fast as possible, or else the meat will go bad. From there, it moves like clockwork. Giancarlo and a coworker are in charge of the cow. First, the beef is halved, then divided into three pieces. Giancarlo shimmies the tip of his knife around the ribs, further separating the carcass. Then, the filleting of the skirt steaks, the thin, striated pieces outlined and lifted off. Next he moves back to the hindquarters, and finally, the chuck. Like a swift surgeon, Giancarlo severs and cleans and organizes the cow.

"One day I want to have my own abattoir," Giancarlo tells me. And he's working his way there, mastering the breakdown of one animal after the next, well on his way to learning how to run his own slaughterhouse. You can see the satisfaction Giancarlo has in his work, the learning and mastery of an age-old custom. Plus, his original goal of figuring out where his food comes from has been satisfied.

Others in the generation are finding a similar satisfaction without purchasing a scimitar. There are a number of butchery classes popping up across the country, amassing lists of eager participants. In New York, The Meat Hook, Fleisher's Pasture-Raised Meats and Dickson's Farmstand Meats all offer Butchery 101 courses—from how to break down an entire steer to how to properly trim a rack of lamb. In Kansas City, Missouri, Millennial butchers slice whole hogs in two while providing detailed instructions for onlookers at East Bottom's Local Pig. 4505 Meats in San Francisco hosts classes on butchery, charcuterie, sausage making and meat cooking techniques. Pupils shell out anywhere from $100 to $1,500 for these fleshy lessons, across the country.

Yet most of us are still in the dark. Even if you're the butcher, there is still a whole lot more to that cow's story. Knowing what the animals are fed, who raised them and where they spend their days would complete the breakdown. Today, we hear stories of pigs being fed liquefied pork remains, cows that subsist almost entirely on corn, chickens that live in such close quarters they sit in each others' feces. Produce is sprayed with pesticides that are contributing to a hyper Darwinian evolution of insects, and doing God knows what to human consumers. Packaged products as simple as cream cheese (which should just be cultured milk) have ingredients including corn syrup solids, modified cornstarch, locust bean gum, guar gum and disodium phosphate.

While many of us escape the cacophony by cooking our own meals and exploring the origins of our food, some need more than that. Some want complete control over what goes into their bodies.

Chapter 5
I'm Gluten-Free. I'm Vegan. I'm Authentic.

During a weekend away from New York, a serendipitous side-trip plunked me down in the right place at the right time: A food festival where the guest of honor was yet another one of my food heroes, Mark Bittman. He was tall and gruff, looking distracted and a bit weary from attention. In his orange polo shirt and khaki pants he could have been any middle-aged Jewish dad from my childhood neighborhood in Chicago. Surrounded by food stalls and eager guests, he politely nodded, sipped and chewed the foods people handed to him. Calming my nerves, I approached. After some praise and chitchat, I quickly laid out my theory about Generation Yum.

"I don't think there's anything different about your generation than the ones before, at least in how you relate to food," he said firmly, referring to stories of his two daughters, one in her 20s, another in her 30s. But his interest was clearly peaked: He offered a full interview a few weeks later at his *The New York Times* office.

Mark Bittman, it could be said, popularized home cooking in the late 1990s. While he didn't revolutionize the kitchen, as Julia Child may have, Bittman simplified it, making it approachable for even the least experienced of cooks. After the modest release of his first cookbook, *Leafy Greens*, in 1995, Bittman published *How to Cook Everything* in 1998, and the rest, they say, is history. The manifesto won the James Beard and Julia Child cookbook awards and was soon an international hit.

Fourteen years later, the self-taught cook is in charge of three columns for *The New York Times* and *The New York Times Magazine*—"Eat," "The Minimalist," and "The Flexitarian"—and a video series for Nytimes.com. He makes regular appearances on *The Today Show*, and writes columns for *Prevention* and *Men's Health*. And then there's his constant stream of new books. After *How to Cook Everything* was a number of follow-ups: *How to Cook Everything Vegetarian*, *How to Cook Everything The Basics*, collaborations with Jean-Georges Vongerichten and more.

A few weeks after our meeting, I found myself in Bittman's office, down the hall from Frank Bruni and a number of other *New York Times* notables, a bag of toasted pepitas balanced in front of us. Since the time we first discussed Gen Yum, the revered food writer, it seemed, had given the topic more thought.

He admitted: Yes, there is more interest in real food today than ever before. Like Bourdain, he commented: "Instagram may be a fad, but people's interest in food is not a fad." He called social media and the restaurant frenzy "an entry point."

Bittman thinks this interest is based in our attempt to overcome a convoluted food system. "Increasingly, people want real food. That is not a fad. Regardless of the point of entry, whether it's because they think animals are cool or they like butchering or they like to eat in restaurants, the interest in food is not going to go away. People are tired of a lack of transparency in what they're eating."

Our generation's interest in vegan, vegetarian and local eating, he believes, is a "response to the processed foods of the last 70 years." One way of coping, he said, is to simplify and regulate your own eating, through trends such as veganism: eliminating all animal product from your diet. But that too, he confesses, is not a complete solution. Even a carrot is no longer just a carrot. Is that a GMO (genetically modified organism) or non-GMO carrot?

Many months after our follow up interview at the *The Times*, halfway through my second year at The New School, Bittman wrote me an email: "What are you doing? M." I wasn't sure how to respond. Is this a *What are you wearing?* kind of situation, I wondered. Thankfully, he wanted to hire me as an assistant, to join his team of two other loyal helpers, one of whom had been by his side for over twelve years, the other, five. Without hesitation, I said yes.

The role was multifaceted: checking Mark's public email account and sending along relevant messages, cutting my teeth on recipe writing and development, meeting with *The New York Times Magazine* art director to receive go-ahead on certain article concepts, chatting with the team at *The Today Show* to coordinate when one dish would come out of the oven and another would go in during Mark's segments. His other assistants and I brainstormed frequently, emailing each other with ideas for the *Times,* hashing out the latest trends, discussing how to translate a great meal Mark had eaten or an awesome chef he'd met into a story. It was a dream. Granted, I was working seven days a week, but I was learning every day.

In the years since *How to Cook Everything,* the food landscape has changed dramatically. More and more people are cooking at home, and the rapid rise in obesity, concerns about global warming and elevated risk of heart disease and diabetes are bringing public attention to the food system. Mark regularly discusses these issues in his op-eds, delving into topics like antibiotics in poultry, the obesity crisis, sugary foods and diet trends. While telling readers how to make gazpacho twelve ways, he also began to toss in heftier messages: *Watch what you're eating, and let's fix the system.*

In short order, his cookbooks began to mirror his new political concerns. In 2008, he released *Food Matters: A Guide to Conscious Eating with More Than 75 Recipes,* and in 2010 a companion cookbook with over 500 recipes. The tone was decidedly different. Instead of tips for broiling shrimp or trimming an artichoke, he zoned in on sustainable eating.

"Could improved health for people and planet be as simple as eating fewer animals, and less junk food and super-refined carbohydrates? Yes," Mark writes. I had purchased *Food Matters* back in D.C. and read it cover to cover. I learned about the rise and risks of industrial farming and sugar consumption, how livestock effects global warming, and ideas on how I could alter my own eating habits to better the planet.

Just months before I was hired, Mark released another book in the same vein: *VB6: Eat Vegan Before 6:00 P.M. to Lose Weight and Restore Your Health . . . for Good.* The message was largely the same as *Food Matters*—what you eat is important for the planet—but this time, the focus was on personal health. Three months into my job with him, I learned about our latest assignment: Write the follow-up cookbook for *VB6*.

The project made perfect sense. Veganism was gaining steam. Bill Clinton announced his relinquishing of animal products, and later Al Gore jumped on board, all touting major weight loss, as Bittman himself had. Michelle Pfeiffer, Carrie Underwood, Russell Brand and Ozzy Osbourne also made their vegan diets public. More and more Americans were limiting their animal product intake. While *Food Matters* put sustainable eating in a global context, *VB6*'s personal and charted diet made it more appealing to the mainstream. Eat this, don't eat that. Feel better. Oh, and by the way, by doing that, you're helping the planet.

I spent the next several months reading through global and healthy eating cookbooks for inspiration, testing veggie burger, sweet potato shepherds pie, avocado chocolate mousse and other imaginative vegan treats in my upgraded five-by-four-foot Brooklyn kitchen. We traded emails and lists of recipe concepts, and tested dozens of vegan and "flexitarian" meals. I saw the eagerness for the cookbook online where we teased the upcoming release. Fans wanted recipes and wanted them fast. The push for veganism, flexitarianism, locavorism and all-natural diets had never been higher. And I was lucky enough to watch it from the inside.

Under Pressure

Twenty young food professionals sat in a horseshoe arrangement at a table with water and a peacock spread of cheese wedges in front of us. Molly, the 30-year-old Wholesale Manager and Menu Consultant at Murray's Cheese in New York City's Greenwich Village, stood before the group with the comfort of an improv actor and the tall stance of a professor. Notice, she advised us, the "oxidized bone color" of one cheese. It's a "clean curd." She twisted around and reached out with a knife to nab a corner of another cheese off her plate. She turned again to face the class and raised the knife to her nose to inhale the scent. "What does it smell like?" she asked us. I stared down at my own slate. "Wet concrete," she offered. "Grapefruit pit and goat." I nodded in agreement with my cohort.

I met Molly for the first time in 2012. A friend had recommended I call her—she would be an interesting Gen Yum subject, they thought. She is frail and fair skinned with a wide smile. As we sat down in the sunny cafe with coffee and quiche before us, I zeroed in on the world of dairy. But the interview turned out to be far more interesting than cheese. Fewer curds and more frank conversation.

"I never learned how to eat," Molly told me of her upbringing. "It was all just to keep the engine running." Molly grew up in Southern Illinois, surrounded by farmland, Walmarts and a top-level state university. Her father is a pastor, her mother, a professor of education. Their home was a mix of food paradigms: A father devoted to farm-to-table and a mother who relied on boxed and frozen meals.

For years, beginning in middle school, Molly refused to eat. As her parents watched her frame shrink beneath sagging clothes, they trusted that she would turn things around herself. She was likely stressed out over the usual anxieties of middle school: weight, friends, school. And she just didn't care that much about food. Except cheese.

Cheese was her weakness. Many nights she'd sneak into the kitchen and melt a block of bright orange cheddar on a plate in the microwave, pull out a fork and eat the entire stringy, pungent treat. Or she'd slice off a rectangle of cream cheese and eat it off the blade, to her mother's disgust. "You can slice it, why can't I eat it that way?" she would say to her mother's disapproving looks. Molly told herself it was her British heritage that allowed her to digest her nearly all-dairy diet.

Her habits changed when a health-focused friend introduced her to the power of food. It was the end of freshman year of high school when Molly met Veronica. They were in *The Wizard of Oz* together. Veronica's dad was into juicing—a totally alien way of food consumption to Molly's upbringing. Molly wanted to keep up with her new friend's *joie de vivre* lifestyle. Ironically, Veronica introduced her to the seven-layer burrito at Taco Bell and soon enough, Molly was eating again. Not just eating, in fact, cooking. She replicated the burritos at home, created black bean burgers and started a job at a juice bar and bagel shop. She surrounded herself with food.

Years later, while working for *Good Housekeeping* as a business manager, Molly decided to take a few of her clients to a cheese class at Murray's. She thought it would be a unique way to get their attention, to spark a conversation. But as the class began, Molly was entranced. She found herself unabashedly shushing her clients. She leaned forward in her chair, and listened to each word the instructor said about protein enzymes and the scent of ammonia that emerges from aging cheeses.

The next time, she went alone and arrived early. The instructor placed that day's cheese selections before her. And then something strange happened. Molly's heart rate quickened, she felt weak, blood rushed to her head. It was as though someone had placed the cutest of puppies in her lap and her skin vibrated with joy. She dipped her head in mortification. Was anyone looking? The piquant cheese had brought her home: home to the open farm air, dirt, animals. It was a visceral connection.

The love affair never ended. She began spending her extra hours outside the office volunteering at the cheese shop so that she could gain free access to their courses. She left work early. She read *The Omnivore's Dilemma* and began thinking more seriously about the way she ate. Eventually, Murray's offered her a job. Eventually, Molly became the manager of cheese sales, cheese cave tours and education classes for the growing company, tasting nearly 80 cheeses per week.

As Molly walked me through her history with food, she bluntly remarked that the food industry is duping us. She blames the lack of connection between industrial food and the earth and our bodies for her own struggles with food and the wider state of food in the United States. She now only eats things with the same birth, life, and deterioration timeline as humans (a.k.a., not the Twinkie or Cool Whip tub that will not mold after sitting out for 20 years). She also readily admits that the control she once felt by limiting the amount of food she consumed has now simply shifted to choosing, very specifically, what she'll put in her body: organic, pesticide-free, preferably local, unprocessed foods.

What Molly practices—organic, locavore eating—has become a trend all its own, like gluten free, vegan, paleo, raw foodist, pescetarian. Eaters are exerting control over what they eat in very particular ways, and it's a socially acceptable, if not celebrated, practice.

On the one hand, I understand Mark and Molly's arguments—that the food system is causing this return to the basics; that paleo, raw foodist trends are the result of, well, a rotten food system. It's so darn hard to know what you're eating, you may as well limit your diet to a few recognizable "real" foods. But I didn't totally buy it. Why now? Why are these trends so huge? While middle-aged Mark Bittman turned to veganism to get his cholesterol down and lose weight, why were a bunch of 25-year-olds following suit? There seemed to be another underlying motivator beyond environmental or health concerns. Namely, control.

What Molly was describing—her interest in very specific foods—and her admission of the satisfaction of controlling her food intake, made me begin to wonder: Is all this restriction just an eating disorder by another name? Are we a generation of disordered eaters?

Molly had connected the two ideas: using food to subdue our ever-growing anxieties as a generation, but taking it a step further from butchering or recipe building to a full-out lifestyle. I began to look around for more evidence of this theory. I came across a presentation by researchers out of Humboldt State University who looked, specifically, at locavore diets. Unlike veganism or the Atkins diet, which exclude certain food groups, locavores are concerned with supporting local agriculture and reducing their carbon footprint by purchasing goods produced within a certain square mileage. This was Molly's ideal—attempting to eat only foods grown as locally as possible.

The researchers hoped to determine the motivations behind locavorism. What they found, after interviewing a dozen subjects, was the running theme of "empowerment":

For most participants, a sense of control emerged not as a result of local food, but out of the *choice* to be local. Many described eating this way as making me "happy"... Interviewee #9 captured this best when he said, "I later learned about the power of food . . . it's pretty liberating to have control over what you eat."

This one example provided evidence that what Molly was expressing—the ability to calm herself through control over her choices, even if that just meant eating food from a certain place—was not an isolated incident. It felt like I had a Gen Yum diagnosis breakthrough.

In the fabulous article by *New York Times* contributor Jessica Bruder, "The Picky Eater Who Came to Dinner," Bruder addresses the "ever-widening array of restrictions" found around the dinner table:

> It's becoming harder for Americans to break bread together. Our appetites are stratified by an ever-widening array of restrictions: gluten free, vegan, sugar free, low fat, low sodium, no carb, no dairy, soyless, meatless, wheatless, macrobiotic, probiotic, antioxidant, sustainable, local and raw.

She shares a story of a woman who was mugged at gunpoint, which led to panic attacks and depression. Then, the subject turned to a gluten, sugar and carb free diet. "Within 48 hours," the woman recalls of beginning her new diet, "it felt like a thick layer of gauze had been pulled off my brain." The regimen, she informed Bruder, acted like an anti-anxiety medication, and it's a habit she relies on whenever she begins to feel uneasy.

In 2006, Petra Sneijder and Hedwig te Molder, two Dutch researchers, looked into behaviors of the online vegan community. They wanted to assess the line between ideology and identity represented in what we choose to eat. What they found would sound strikingly familiar to anyone with knowledge of eating disorders—a community that repeatedly tried to normalize its behavior by suggesting the ordinariness of its choices: Vegan meals are simple! You can avoid vitamin deficiency by doing these three things! To summarize, the report states that subjects were presenting themselves, "as a gourmet to counter accusations of being an unhealthy eater."

One of the most common food fads today is the gluten-free diet. Gluten is a protein found most commonly in bread products. You also may know it as seitan, used to make mock meats. In the last several years, a growing number of concerned eaters have declared themselves "gluten intolerant" or "gluten sensitive." In fact, today, 18 million people report discomfort after eating gluten, and 29 percent of American adults say they're trying to cut back on or completely avoid gluten in their diets.

Common gluten-free products—like popcorn, rice Chex and mixed nuts—now taut their gluten-freeness on packaging. In 2013 customers ordered more than 200 million—yes, 200 million!—advertised gluten or wheat-free restaurants items. Sales of gluten-free products will exceed $15 billion dollars by 2016, doubling since 2011. (If only there was a gluten free stock…)

So what's changed about gluten? Why are recordings of "gluten sensitivity" just now on the rise? Perhaps there's an upsurge in gluten in our processed food? A new form of gluten? In 2014, writer Michael Specter attempted to answer the question "What's So Bad About Gluten?" for *The New Yorker.*

"Everyone is trying to figure out what is going on, but nobody in medicine, at least not in my field, thinks this adds up to anything like the number of people who say they feel better when they take gluten out of their diet," Joseph A. Murray explains to Specter. Murray is a professor of medicine at the Mayo Clinic and the president of the North American Society for the Study of Celiac Disease who has also studied wheat genetics (a.k.a. pretty darn qualified to speak on the issue). "It's hard to put a number on these things, but I would have to say that at least seventy per cent of it is hype and desire. There is just nothing obviously related to gluten that is wrong with most of these people."

"I've been gluten-free these last four years, and it has changed my life," Marie Papp, a photographer, tells Specter. "I would have headaches, nausea, trouble sleeping. I know that I'm intolerant because I gave it up and I felt better. That explanation is probably not scientific enough for you. But I know how I felt, how I feel, and what I did to make it change."

Specter remained confused. The scientists were telling him nothing was wrong with these people, but the gluten intolerant folks he met insisted otherwise. Then, Specter heard a story about a friend's wife who went to a psychiatrist to treat feelings of depression and anxiety. The psychiatrist prescribed a gluten-free diet. It was exactly as Molly had described, and what Bruder's subject had also expressed: simplified eating habits as an anti-anxiety method.

"We are seeing more and more cases of orthorexia nervosa," Peter H. R. Green, the director of the celiac-disease center at the Columbia University medical school explains to Specter, discussing the method of progressively abstaining from specific foods. "First, they come off gluten. Then corn. Then soy. Then tomatoes. Then milk. After a while, they don't have anything left to eat—and they proselytize about it."

The strangest part, Green notes—beyond the lack of scientific evidence that gluten is detrimental to our physical health (with the exception of celiac disease, which only affects one percent of the population)—is that many of the gluten-free foods dieters are eating as substitutions are highly processed foods, made with blends of starches, refined carbohydrates and tons of sugar—basically, foods that are, without a doubt, bad for them. "Our patients have jumped on this bandwagon and largely left the medical community wondering what the hell is going on," Green says.

It's all about the comfort of control. Bagels are perhaps not the culprit, but the growing anxieties and depression within Generation Y. While cooking at home soothes Cate and Giancarlo finds solace in expertly breaking down a steer, others find that sense of calm through controlling daily food choices.

Gen Yum faces numerous anxiety-provoking factors: the barrage of constant buzzes and dings that demand immediate attention; a lack of face-to-face human connection; high unemployment rates, low pay; the management of the in-person and avatar identities; and general confusion over the functioning of our ever-more complicated technologically-infused environments. And yes, perhaps our a sketchy food system and the plague of too many choices are also driving Gen Yum's out-of-the-ordinary food choices.

While options are at the core of the American experiment (I like my Frappucino tall, lite, mocha, no whip, please), study after study has shown that too many choices puts you into a phase of perpetual fear. We only have the cognitive capacity to make so many decisions a day, and each little one depletes our ability to stay sharp. Yet in today's society, choices are rampant.

I began to think about the chaos of everyday life and the calm created by reducing our choices. This theory is nothing new, of course. In fact, it was made famous in the 2000 "jam study" in which researchers presented some participants with 24 jam choices, others, only six. Those shown 24 jams were far less likely to make a jam purchase, too overwhelmed by the options and stressed about making a correct decision. Those with less choice were more satisfied with their decisions. Lesson learned? We like being able to decide, but too many options are like a buffet. No one is ever pleased.

A coworker recently told me that a few months on the ketone—or ketogenic—diet allowed him to sleep better; his stress levels were down. He mainly ate meat and cheese. One day I heard him declare that he was only eating almonds. Bread and its affiliates were out the window. Vegetables played a big role. It was Atkins with even more protein. "That's interesting," I said to him, "but do you really think that eating tons of animal protein is what made you feel better?" He seemed baffled. Restricting one's eating, accomplishing a goal, simplifying just one part of your life, I suggested, might have actually played the true beneficial role in that diet. The pounds, after all, come back almost immediately when dieters take a break. High ketone levels can cause nausea and bad breath, and high protein diets raise cholesterol and can cause a number of other health risks. I could tell I'd offended him—he was certain it was the foods that had caused the change. I dropped my case, at least with him.

There's nothing shameful in longing for simplicity and control. It's what we crave—and what, more than ever, we're lacking. We live in a world stuffed with intricate technologies, unstable economic systems, and a plethora of choices. Carl Richards called it "The Trap of Too Many Choices" in the *New York Times,* citing author Barry Schwartz's *Paradox of Choice*:

> "When people have no choice, life is almost unbearable …. But as the number of choices keeps growing, negative aspects of having a multitude of options begin to appear … the negatives escalate until we become overloaded. At this point, choice no longer liberates, but debilitates. It might even be said to tyrannize."

Today, we choose which online store to frequent, which TV series is worth binge watching, which aggregator site will come up with the cheapest flight, on top of considerations more familiar to previous generations: which stock to invest in, which route to take to work. Just entering the cereal aisle is enough to set off a panic attack.

This reaction is sensible for a generation where one-fifth of us have been diagnosed with depression. Reports show that many Millennials report feelings of helplessness, hopelessness, passivity, boredom, fear, isolation and dehumanization, resulting in a loss of autonomy and community connection. (Antidepressants are the most frequently used class of medications by

Americans ages 18 to 44 years old.) We are primed to perform behaviors that will give us just a bit of autonomy and community back.

Many of these new "diets" reflect common disordered eating symptoms. The difference is that *these* habits are out in the open—admired, even, because they run in parallel with wider areas of concern: fixing our food system. As Molly struggled with anorexia, her parents remained silent. Today, she chides her family for not eating organic or local. Her food choices are a point of pride, not embarrassment or concern. And the same goes for many of the "picky" eaters Bruder highlights in her witty essay: "Today's restricted eaters are prone to identity-driven pronouncements along the lines of 'I'm gluten free.' (It's worth noting that, back in the aughts, no one declared 'I'm Atkins!' Except, quite possibly, Dr. Robert Atkins himself.)"

Just like our Instagrammed lunches and trips to the farmer's markets, our restrictive diets have become a new identifier. People introduce themselves by eating habits in profiles. (I.e. "I'm a vegan raw foodist from Ojai, CA" or a "pescetarian environmentalist from Ontario.")

Today, perhaps because of its pervasiveness and the glow of food activism, the shame in restricted one's eating has been significantly lowered. You still don't want to be the person who says, "I don't eat." But it's perfectly acceptable to say, "I don't eat gluten or any animal products."

We may be going vegan or paleo out of a frustration with the lack of transparency in our food. But again, a similar situation already played out in the 1960s when Rachel Carson's *Silent Spring* revealed the truth about DDT. Then, those who took on a pesticide-free, vegetarian lifestyle were, without a doubt, on the fringe. Today, being a paleo locavore is hip. Going gluten free is easy. Avoiding soy? Not a problem. So while I'd like to agree with Mark— that this is really all just a benevolent and worldly-minded decision about wanting whole foods—I actually think—for the vast majority of Yummers— it's also related to emotions tied up in things entirely unrelated to what we eat.

That Place is Supposed to be Super Authentic

"Authentic" was one of the words I began to hear more and more around 2012. "Oh, that place has the most authentic mole," I would hear. "I want 'authentic' Chinese, not *American* Chinese" (said with a slight sneer).

Even Anthony Bourdain isn't immune: "If I see non-Japanese behind the sushi bar, there's a little voice in my head saying no, no, no, no, no." But, "if it's a filthy bathroom and there's a chicken in the dining room, I start feeling like I'm at an authentic place too, you know?"

No one wants a Nicaraguan rolling his or her sushi. They want the guy who has just stepped off Air Japan. They don't want a restaurant covered in fake Aztec art. They want a hole-in-the-wall Peruvian joint. They want the real thing.

But authenticity is tricky. What is authentic to me may not be authentic to you. Most crucially, it has little to do with all the other factors mentioned above: whether something is produced responsibly, whether it is good for your body or the earth or even whether it tastes good.

In *Authenticity: What Consumers Really Want*, authors James Gilmore and Joseph Pine write that, "in industry after industry, in customer after customer, authenticity has overtaken quality as the prevailing purchasing criterion." Much ink has been spilled on understanding the Millennial generation for marketing purposes. Everyone wants the answer to consumer demands. Authenticity appears to be one.

I called Francis Lam to get his take. A shrewd and phrenic conversation between Francis and Eddie Huang had recently been published on *Gilt Taste* (sadly, taken down when the site went under), where they debated issues of identity and origin in food.

"It's the most loaded word," Francis said during our meeting on the West Side, referring to "authenticity." Francis is now an editor-at-large at Clarkson Potter. He made his career in food journalism as a senior writer at *Salon* and a contributing editor at *Gourmet*. We met in Hell's Kitchen to hash out the etymology of authenticity.

"Is it authentic that you're a graphic designer but you sold your studio to move to Vermont to become a cheese maker, and three years later you're living the life of a master craftsman or craftswoman cheese maker when you really just picked it up three years ago? Is that authentic?"

Francis talked about the uniquely American desire to categorize food by national cuisine (a.k.a. "I want Chinese food," versus "I want fried rice"), and now, by levels of authenticity.

"Whatever authenticity is trying to mean is probably wrong, right? And that's fine. The world's a big place," he said, suggesting that what most of us think of as "authentic" Mexican or "authentic" Indian are likely anything but. "If someone says, 'Is this going to be authentic Chinese cuisine?' I kind of know what you're getting at when you say that but what do you really mean as authentic? Is it authentic cuisine to China, because China's really big and there are like eight official regional cuisines, and then each town and each cook. Is it authentic to 2013 or is it authentic to 1913 or 1484? That pursuit of authenticity is the rabbit hole that never ends. You can drive yourself looking for something truly authentic. At the same time the word means something because everyone uses it and everyone is trying to get it."

In 2012, I attended a food conference at New York University where researcher Balázs Kovács spoke about a study that evaluates what the common consumer deems "authentic," and whether or not we place higher value on foods and restaurants considered as such.

"I'm not really sure I know what authenticity is," Kovács confessed. Nevertheless, he says, the notion is gaining more and more value in American society. The researchers wanted to know if their subjects could agree on a definition of authentic food and whether subjects spent more money on a food deemed "authentic." Words associated with authenticity include "genuine," "real," "skilled," "faithful," "legitimate," "original," "tradition." Against authenticity: "imitation," "quack," "unreal," "imposter." They searched for commonalities between restaurants deemed "authentic."

In the first study, the researchers evaluated over 1.2 million Yelp reviews written between 2004 and 2011 in Los Angeles, New York and Dallas. The second study presented participants with images and short descriptions of fictitious restaurants. The subjects were then asked to rate the made-up restaurant's authenticity.

They found that restaurants considered "authentic" were more likely to have higher ratings, even after the researchers controlled for the restaurant's quality in other ways—food, price and age of the establishment. They also found that consumers "perceive independent, family-owned and specialist (single-category) restaurants as more authentic than they do chain, non-family-owned and generalist (multiple-category) restaurants."

"Higher decor ratings lead to lower ratings on Yelp," Kovács explained. "If you're an authentic restaurant, you can get away with being dirty," he reported, referencing food carts and open kitchens. Un-American (in its most stereotypical interpretation) is the most authentic.

When reports have shown that a one star increase in Yelp ratings leads to a five to nine percent increase in revenue for that restaurant, it seems all restaurants should want consumers to view them as authentic.

Why do we think that a dubiously clean papusa joint with a mother in the kitchen is actually better than a restaurant with chi-chi decor that likely brings in fresh ingredients every day? It's not about the food at all—it's about honesty, or the perception of it.

"The demand for authenticity—the honest or the real—is one of the most powerful movements in contemporary life, influencing our moral outlook, political views, and consumer behavior," writes Andrew Potter in *The Authenticity Hoax: How We Get Lost Finding Ourselves.*

"Authenticity is a rebellion against modernity," Kovács explained to a captivated audience. "You want to go back to your roots, what's real or true, you want to go back to that, even it's not that interesting, even if it's imaginary, you want to go back to that." That urge to return to simplicity is so strong that we're willing to choose one taco joint over another based solely on its perceived authenticity. It means comfort and nostalgia. It is home (even if you grew up in a middle class, English speaking, suburban home). It's not about the type of food, but the food experience. Bob White's small New York eatery with 20 seats and the owner serving you sweet-tea brined fried chicken is deemed authentic. A few blocks over, Blue Ribbon's latest joint where you see buckets of fried chicken piled under heat lamps is considered trendy, but not authentic. The taste of the chicken itself is almost irrelevant—the atmosphere is what qualifies or disqualifies a joint in its ranking of authenticity.

It all comes back to the drive for simplicity, connection and control—things that are increasingly hard to come by in our urban environments in particular. To cope, we devise other systems for ourselves: We seek out authentic meals, search for USDA organic ingredients, call our friends to share a meal at home and learn about the places our ingredients come from. But for some, even this is not enough. In fact, some are leaving the cities altogether and finding authenticity in other places, swapping digging into a plate of chicken for digging into the dirt.

Chapter 6
Mom and Dad, I'm Moving to a Farm

They settled into creaking homes along the hillsides of Northeast Vermont, woven between farmland, placid lakes and areas of spotty cell reception. On their own, they planned and organized, mowed and harvested, and installed wifi. They came to this hidden valley of artisans and thinkers with their own goals and motivations, their own ideas of who they wanted to be. For most, it was the start of adulthood.

In the last few years, handfuls of young entrepreneurs have flocked to the calm, scenic area known as the Northeast Kingdom. Some were leaving their city jobs, others returning home. Seemingly all have impressive college or graduate school degrees in hand and parents looking on in confusion.

My research into the Millennial generation had taken me high and low—from underground restaurants to hors d'oeuvres with Anthony Bourdain; from D.C.'s developing restaurant scene to the booming culinary metropolis of New York; from cheese caves to pondering our Gen Yum's psychological conundrums. But there was still a critical part of the phenomenon I was completely missing: Gen Yummers who don't care about the latest restaurant or getting the best angle for their Instagram photo, but knowing what's in season, when to harvest and the land around them. Cooks I was familiar with. But farmers? Not so much.

During a routine afternoon of Internet wanderings, I came across an article about Taylor Cocalis, co-founder of the job search-engine Good Food Jobs. She seemed like a great representative of middle-of-the-road Millennials: raised in the suburbs of New Jersey, college at Cornell, graduate school at the University of Gastronomic Sciences in Italy (ok, here's where it starts to veer), former cheese-class coordinator at Murray's Cheese in New York City (yes, where Molly works), and now, supportive fiancé, teacher and website owner, living in that oddly-titled locale, The Kingdom. After calling Taylor to hear her story, I quickly realized that she would became my introduction to this farm-centric cohort: those who turn off the television, get up from their desks and don't just dig their hands into a bowl of batter, but devote themselves to physical labor and earthly connection.

Days after interviewing Taylor on the phone, I wrote to ask if I could come stay with her. A calendar page later, I was sitting around her living room table with Taylor herself, her fiancé Daniel, her roommate Zoe and Zoe's boyfriend Shaun.

When I entered their white countryside home, I saw an enormous leg of lamb marinating on the counter, smothered with crème fraîche, garlic, lemon and mint picked from the small batch of herbs planted alongside the bottom porch step—thyme, green and purple basil, rosemary. I arrived just as Taylor and Daniel were beginning their prep for dinner. Daniel worked as a brewer at Hill Farmstead Brewery, operated and owned by fellow young beer-aphile Shaun Hill. Daniel is short and thin and on that day his bushy, thick brown hair was reaching impressive heights. His shirt was stained and ripped, I assumed from managing and cleaning the 20 feet tall brew tanks. He lit the grill and after setting the leg atop the flame, returned indoors and flipped open his Mac to search for more firewood on Craigslist and send an email to a local farmer to see when he could come by to purchase a bunch of chickens.

As we waited for the perfect char, Taylor took me to the garden to gather vegetables for coleslaw. Stalks of broccoli and kale and vines of squash weaved through a patch of soil alongside their home, emerging in perfectly squared off patches like a Mondrian painting. We were looking for carrots. I knelt in the garden, inspecting the leaves on the carrot tops to guess their relative size beneath the soil, but I had no idea what I was supposed to be looking for. The first few I pulled were premature, no bigger than a thumb. Taylor waved off my apologies. I'd never picked my own dinner before.

Did You Say Desk Job?

Taylor is tall and lanky, with a boisterous laugh. She's almost frustratingly positive, and could be easily mistaken for a routine, feckless Millennial. But that would be a far cry from reality. Taylor and a friend co-own a successful job search site, Good Food Jobs, where food-minded folks can search a diverse set of job listings—from line cooks to food startup community managers. Inspiration for the company came while Taylor was working as a cheese expert at Murray's. There, she observed that the young professionals—like Molly—who attend their courses were expressing a "deep desire to do something that they really believed in."

"Everyone was really unsure how to navigate between what was expected of them and/or the types of salaries they were making and hours they were working," Taylor told me over the phone before my arrival. Many wished to leave their nine-to-five corporate jobs, but were also afraid. 60 to 80 people came in to volunteer once or twice a month to help set up and break down the classroom for the cheese courses. People kept saying, "I really love food and you really seem to have just attacked this and really love what you're doing. I want to know how to do that as well." Eventually, her informal role as life coach for the various corporate workers inspired her to start Good Food Jobs.

"There's a weird shift I keep seeing," Taylor said. "For older age groups, there's a stigma surrounding working in food. Recently, a woman told me of her friend's son who just graduated from college with a psychology degree and declared he wants to be a farmer. His parents are distraught. It was an appalling idea that someone would want to do manual, physical labor. But there's a generation of us now that are really into it and we actually crave these tangible things," she explained emphatically.

"Our culture sets these weird expectations about the jobs we're supposed to have," she continued, when asked about the success of her thriving business. "People tell us the things we should be doing, but those expectations aren't necessarily rooted in anything real. I mean, yeah, I can work magic on an Excel spreadsheet, but I can't build anything. Last week I bought a circular saw and I had to YouTube how to use it to cut lumber to build some potato towers." Taylor thinks we're all just craving a bit more reality, plus, she said, "We've seen what happened with our parent's generation. It all seems surreal—the amount of money they were able to make so quickly, and this idea that the pinnacle is that you make more and more money doing less and less work. There's a backlash now. We've seen that it's not sustainable. And it doesn't exercise your creativity. Folks are looking for something that's more tangible and rooted and real." And food, especially farming, is just that.

United States farm culture is in a period of transition. The average age of the American farmer is nearly 60. Children who grew up on farms are flocking to urban centers, to jobs that don't depend on the whims of Mother Nature. According to the organization Young Farmers, the number of American farmers has steadily declined over the last century, from over six million in 1910 to just over two million in 2007. The number of farms in the

U.S. declined by four percent between 2007 and 2012, leaving about 2.1 million in operation today. For each farmer under 35 years old, there are six over 65. With so many farmers reaching retirement age, it is estimated that between now and 2030, half a million (one quarter) of American farmers will retire. This could cause major problems economically, environmentally and socially. "The success of beginning farmers today will determine the quality of food we eat, the future of our rural landscapes and the longevity of our farming traditions," states the Young Farmers report.

The young people who once would have taken over the family farm no longer want that responsibility or uncertainty. "It's a very rare person who's not grown up on a farm that's going to go out and say, 'I want to plant 100,000 acres of corn. I want to invest $300,000 in a tractor. I want to get a confinement hog barn with 300,000 pigs,'" remarks farmer Eva Teague to NPR. But here's the thing: That's exactly what's happening. In a 2011 survey by the National Young Farmers' Coalition, 78 percent of the 1,300 respondents said they hadn't grown up on a farm, and most were between the ages of 25 and 29. These numbers do not yet offset the anticipated blow of the retiring agricultural cohort, but it's a start.[xvii]

Taylor is part of a growing young population in the Northeast Kingdom. Alongside farmlands and Sterling College—with its new Rian Fried Center for Sustainable Agriculture and Food Systems—are a number of food-centric businesses including Caledonia Spirits, Hill Farmstead Brewery, The Cellars at Jasper Hill Farm and High Mowing Seeds, one of the leading businesses for organic seeds in the United States. You don't have to drive more than five miles to learn to make gin, beer, creamy cheeses, cured meats, or even apprentice to be a farmer.

Farming is gaining such steam among urbanites nationwide that "organic farmers who used to spend part of the winter recruiting workers for the next summer now are turning people away," reports NPR. An annual organic farming conference at Dan Barber's Stone Barns, a nonprofit farm and education center just north of New York City, sells out months in advance—just like a reservation at their restaurant, Blue Hill, in the West Village. Organic farming is becoming the hot topic, a title to tout.

Finally it was time to eat. Zoe, Shaun, Dan, Taylor and I gathered around the living room table, some of us on the couch, others kneeling on the floor. Taylor had tossed the chopped cabbage, yellow and orange carrots, and forest green broccoli with crème fraîche, mayonnaise, lemon and piri piri sauce to make a sparkling plate of coleslaw. I tasted the sugars and bitters and meatiness found in a raw vegetable, harvested minutes before. We drank Hill Farmstead's golden Walden brew from the tap in the living room corner, dubbed "the booze nook." The TV was covered with a large red blanket. A wide window framed the dusk-darkening mountain view. Shaun and Dan spent most of the evening discussing yeast strains and water conditions for their latest brew. Later, they filled shot glasses with Barr Hill honey gin given to them by a neighbor—they couldn't quite remember, but it was probably in exchange for cheese from Jasper Hill, where Zoe works.

I was worried I'd feel out of place, surrounded by people my age who had chosen a different path. But it wasn't so. These young entrepreneurs, farmers and thinkers had grown up just like me, our childhoods colored by Monica Lewinsky, 9/11, Tamagotchi and Michael Jordan. They love Beyoncé and voted for Obama. These were my people. These were Yummers. They just knew how to farm.

Time To Dig In

On my second day in Vermont, I visited another young transplant to the area, Annie Myers. Annie arrived in Craftsbury, Vermont in the winter of 2010, when the cold air made the blue and white tarps in the fields dip in deep frowns, frosted the washbins in the kitchen and lined the freezer with white furry ice. Her first assignment at Pete's Greens Organic Vegetable Farm was to wash produce in the bitterly frigid metal sinks.

On this decidedly warmer July afternoon, Annie wore faded jean shorts, cut off and frayed. Her Birkenstocks were all but camouflaged with dust. Her arms and legs were decorated with scrapes and scars, mementos of her time pulling weeds and harvesting with "the amigos," as she calls them, a temporary crew of six Mexican field workers. Once a resident of New York City's Greenwich Village, Annie brought me into the vegetable beds, pulling and tasting as she roamed. "I don't really have a lot of farming skills," she informed me, checking to see if her boss was nearby, though later she clarified that she is, of course, a farmer.

Annie explained her journey to Pete's Greens, where she was working six days a week, usually from dawn to dusk. She managed the harvest crew and inventory, and worked with the wholesale buyers and CSA pickups. She also decideed when the produce was ready for harvest. Four days a week she was in the field collecting a range of organic vegetables, including kale, sweet potatoes, a variety of beans, tomatoes and salad greens.

Raised by a financial advisor, with five siblings who work in banking, medicine and education, she said that her parents don't understand her choice of profession. "Maybe it's going to take you into politics," her mother has suggested.

After years of home schooling and boarding school, Annie decided to spend time in Italy after high school graduation through WWOOF (the World Wide Opportunities on Organic Farms). She lived with an Italian family—parents and two sons—that hosted her for three months in exchange for her labor. She thought it would be a great way to learn Italian. In the end, she could not only speak some Italian, but had also learned how to make wine and pick olives. "It was the most bucolic, wonderful thing I've ever done," she told me. I imagine her stooped down in a row of wine grapes, shadowed by the vines from the setting Umbrian sun.

Annie enrolled at New York University to study journalism, and worked to integrate her fascination with food and food systems into her life through various volunteer positions. After graduation, she hop-scotched through a series of jobs with highly esteemed food mavens in New York, including Robert Lavalva, who started New Amsterdam Market, Anne Saxelby of Saxelby Cheesemongers and Jake Dickson of Dickson's Farmstead Meats, before working at chef April Bloomfield's acclaimed Spotted Pig as New York City's first official restaurant forager. *New York Magazine* called Annie a "hunter-gatheress" in a profile. But Annie was unfulfilled. Each of her jobs had been peripheral: working the counter or collecting goods on someone else's checklist. "I'm super interested in distribution," she told me, "the best way get food to people in the city, and now just the best way to get food to people anywhere."

Remembering Pete's Greens from a brief visit to Vermont years prior, Annie picked up the phone and called Pete to ask for a job. Though she recalls wondering why anyone would want to live in Craftsbury, a town with little more than a post office and general store, she knew the farm was open year-round and had an efficient form of distribution. Plus, her itch to dig her hands into something, literally, was getting to her.

Two years later, she walked the fields, inspecting the harvest. She drove me to Pete's new rented fields and disappeared behind the walls of waving corn stalks. She emerged minutes later, cradling four ears, peeled back the tops and sampled the kernels. She handed me the sweetest cob, and we leaned against the car hood, devouring the raw bounty.

"I really enjoy having a substantive product that you end your day with. I was telling Dan the other day, 'I went through thousands of pounds of food today, I pulled it out of the field and I brought it in and like, I feel it and I held it and people are eating it,' versus feeling like all you produced were emails. It's a really satisfying feeling. It's very tangible. You're a part of it."

"A lot of what there is to learn, you can't really learn from a book. I've been picking melons right now," she explains, "I can't tell you how much, having done it last year, and cried over it, been yelled at over it, picked them at the wrong time, the next year you get it a little better. I know what they're supposed to sound like when you knock 'em. It's awesome. It's not something you can tell someone how to do."

Annie is not alone: Many Millennials are learning to drive tractors, weed and sow seeds because it's satisfying, and it's *hard*. Farming requires extensive knowledge in botany and engineering. "We have a brain flow going to farms and food work," Michael Pollan told Adam Platt in *New York Magazine*. "Some of the smartest people I know are farmers, and chefs, and brewers, and cheesemakers."

In fact, farming has inspired recent public school curricula, which use greenhouses to teach students about photosynthesis, cell structure, weather, atmosphere and the physics of energy, starting in elementary school.

Farming is profoundly practical. You can hedge your bets on whether the latest tech company will change the world, but food will always be in demand. You work and you make something that you can see and feel and, hopefully, eat.

In 2012, *The New York Times* profiled several elite college graduates who had become farmers. One of their subjects, Calvin Kyrkostas, who graduated from Oberlin College, noted his addiction "to the feeling of accomplishment that came with seeing—and eating—the fruits of his labor after 15-hour workdays."

Another recent grad, Abe Bobman, who studied sociology at Wesleyan University, told the *Times*: "Farming appeals to me, and probably to other people, because it's simple and straightforward work outdoors with literal fruits from your labor. It doesn't feel like you're a part of an oppressive institution."

Gen Yummers want to have actual skills. Like, survival skills. Or just skills that aren't reliant on digital technology. This also puts *us* in control. Look around and you'll note the return to craftsmanship not just on the farm but also in restaurants and artist coops around the country. Professions that were once considered lower class are now in fashion. If your grandfather made furniture, we know he was probably blue collar. Today, the *Post* profiles "furniture makers that are true tastemakers."

Gen Yers are creating hand-made stationary, artisanal perfumes, and pickles of all varieties. With the job market in a free fall during our post-college years, starting our own businesses—or at least having something creative to do after getting home from the temp agency—appealed. Can't find a job? Make one. Some of us are creating apps and tech startups; others have turned to voguish hands-on endeavors—like farming.

The trend is threefold: A return to nature feels meaningful, allows Yummers to exert control over their seeded product, and—just as important—is a small "screw you" to societal expectations. This growing population of educated Americans is turning to our computer-strapped society and saying, "Hey, you guys have this all wrong. Let me show you how it could be." They are rebelling against the standards that have been placed on our generation—the expectations that were impossible to fulfill in a collapsed marketplace and an entrenched, cynical political system. We don't want to sit in an office connected to our phones and computers and televisions (unless we're looking at food as an escape). And we certainly don't want to replicate the errors of the Boomer generation.

This trend may seem like a callback to the counterculture movement of the late 1960s and early '70s: A new interest in organic foods; the "Diggers," who used food as a means to build "collective social consciousness and social action" in San Francisco. They "saw food as a means to circumvent the military-industrial establishment and build an alternative system of nourishing the masses," writes David Kamp in *The United States of Arugula.*

'I think the big moment really is the 1960s counterculture, when the counterculture holds up the industrial white bread as an icon of everything they oppose," remarked Aaron Bobrow-Strain, at a reading of his book *White*

Bread: A Social History of the Store-Bought Loaf. "It's plastic, it's chemical, it's corporate, it's bland, it's suburban."

The 1969 Santa Barbara oil spill and worries about DDT, world hunger and natural disasters inspired many restricted diets, including macrobiotic, vegetarianism and veganism. "1968 and 1969 were years when it was hard to feel confident in planetary survival," writes Warren Belasco in *Appetite for Change: How the Counterculture Took On the Food Industry.* Natural, whole food was the antithesis of war, politics and rapidly developing technologies.

But I was hearing motivations that were less political and far more personal. Just as I hadn't heard overwhelming woes about Monsanto from locavores, but personal needs being fulfilled by eating a certain way. This wasn't about saving the world or avoiding the draft. This was about living the best life possible.

That night, with Zoe and Shaun at work, Annie joined Taylor, Dan and me for dinner. She was wearing a white Spotted Pig t-shirt and mismatched earrings; dirt lines remained beneath her freshly washed fingernails. That night, we ate farm fresh yellow corn (now cooked), brined chicken and kale Caesar salad. "If you're not going to brine, don't even fucking bother," Dan advised. Taylor served vanilla ice cream with chocolate shavings. They asked me about my impressions so far.

"It's really different," I remarked, than my day-to-day in the city.

"I feel like we all do the same things that we would be doing in New York," Taylor said. *But what about your vegetable garden? Being woken by cows? Driving on a gravel path?* "That's true," she admitted.

"My entire life is not one I could lead in New York," Annie stated. She laughed at the notion that her life in Vermont was anything like her life in New York City.

I Can Kill That Myself, Thank You

Over dinner, Annie, Dan and Taylor asked what I'd be doing with the remainder of my visit. I told them that my next stop was to visit Pete Colman, the owner of Vermont Salumi, a meat producer.

As I said Pete's name, Annie tilted her head slightly and the two girls let out audible sighs. "Oh you're going to see Pete?" Annie's eyes rolled up.

"What's with the look?" I asked.

"Have you seen him?" Annie questioned. "Just wait until you spend time with him. You'll see."

Sure enough, within seconds of meeting Pete, the Casanova charm came shining through. I got it. The longer I looked at him, the more I understood their comparisons to Jude Law in skinny jeans. He leaned against the wall like a Playgirl pinup: farmer edition.

We talked meat. Pete was living in a building on his parent's farm. But unlike a typical apartment, this one had just undergone renovations to add a meat processing area: metal tables, a cooler with meat hooks and a saw. Behind the meat grinder, a window looks out onto his living room: fireplace and desk, red cushioned chair and rows of records stacked inside worn wooden bookshelves. His bedroom is tucked off to the side. Next to the meat room is his kitchen; a beautiful carved table covered in fleur-de-lis and zigzagging lines is his main prep area, topped with a bowl of vegetables, toaster oven, espresso maker and coffee grinder. Pots of dried out herbs hung from the ceiling—Pete couldn't identify them until he pinched a wilting plant and, rubbing it between his fingers, sniffed. "Sage," he determined.

Pete was born in Umbria, Italy, but relocated to Montpelier, Vermont with his mother at the age of three. Raised on his stepfather's organic vegetable farm, Pete spent his years post high school bouncing between summers harvesting at the farm, winters serving cafeteria-style food at a ski resort in Utah and eventually working for a wood manufacturer back home. In between, he would spend a few weeks each year back in Italy with his grandparents.

One day, as Pete puts it, "throwing back" prosciutto with his grandparents, he announced: "I want to learn how to make this stuff." The local butcher encouraged Pete to apprentice with his brother, Francesco, who slaughtered and cured meats himself.

The experience "blew my fucking mind," Pete said. "It's real. There's nothing fancy about it. This is stuff that's been going on for thousands of years." When he returned to the U.S., Pete purchased three pigs. He raised them, slaughtered them, and "did my best not to fuck it up." It was his first attempt in making the meats he admired. *Prosciutto, coppa cola, lanza, guanciale, salami, pancetta, mazzafegato*; Pete listed them, waving his hands as he spoke—a true Italian at heart.

I admired a bone candleholder. He told me his girlfriend made it. "It's good that you like it," he said. "You're attracted to it." He relayed a conversation he had with his girlfriend the night before about the satisfaction of touching flesh. He was standing in the kitchen, leaning against the etched wooden table. I sat on a stool on the other side, sipping a strong espresso he had prepared for me.

"I love touching meat. When I was growing up I loved having my hands on it...It's very tangible, very real," he said as he leaned against the counter. He attributed the positive sensations to the strong smells of a carcass. It's "visceral." He compared killing to sex and eating—the animalistic, elements of life—careful to assure me he is not turned on by killing.

"I feel like it's a religious experience for sure," Pete said of butchering. "There's something really amazing that happens in between that slaughter from the live animal, to dying then scalded or skinned." He said that hunger pains don't hit until the animal is hanging on the hook. "I think it's important for people to kill," he said. Society needs a healthy outlet for this very instinctual desire. "Killing has been part of our culture forever, but we just don't do it now. No one kills anything."

With the displacement of both birth and death from the home into the hospital institution—not to mention the convenience and sanitation of supermarket shopping, so far from the reality of the slaughterhouse—the life/death cycle has been marginalized in contemporary American life. I have friends who won't eat anything with a head because it reminds them that their dinner was once alive. Some Gen Yummers, both on and off the farm, don't want to distance themselves from the origins of their food any longer.

"In May 2011," reports *The New York Times,* Mark Zuckerberg, founder of Facebook "made a pledge to consume, for one year, only meat he had hunted or slaughtered himself. He got a hunting license and shot a bison. 'My personal challenge,' he explained, is 'being thankful for the food I have to eat.'" (Ironic that the king of social media has vowed to only eat what he kills?)

Killing what you eat is growing in popularity, not just on farmland like Pete's, but for urbanites gone wild. "They want to thoughtfully stare their protein in the face, to take locavorism to blood-flecked new heights," notes Dwight Garner in the *Times,* mocking hipster hunters as "J. Crew-wearing Natty Bumppos." Lily Raff McCaulou, author of *Call of the Mild: Learning to*

Hunt My Own Dinner, left her job as a movie director's personal assistant to pursue an interest in hunting, purchasing a shotgun and learning gun safety before working her way up to slaughtering a full sized elk. "Thank you, I'm sorry," she apologizes to each kill.

Either this trend is taking the desire to break things down, to understand what we're consuming, to a whole new level—even being a butcher isn't quite enough—or it's the most extreme way to remind oneself that we are simply animals on this planet, living among other living things, connected somehow. Either way, stopping the heart of a deer and bringing it home to butcher is just about as far away from texting as you can get.

Each night at dinner I watched as Taylor, Dan and the friends who had joined us, gossiped about the usual things, you know: which farmer had better livestock, what temperature tomatoes like best, what produce to expect the next week—watermelons were coming in at Pete's. Taylor and Daniel were planning their wedding; Annie was on the hunt for the ever-elusive boyfriend. As I woke in the mornings from Daniel rushing out of the house as the clock ticked past seven and cows mooed outside my window, I felt a world away from home. But I began to see myself in these energetic, idealistic young people. I even asked myself, *Did I wish to live on a farm?* Maybe one day.

But then I thought about going home. How could I eat this way in New York? Why couldn't most people afford these delicious, organic vegetables I was eating every day, plucked right from the ground? Pete had complained about the strict regulations on selling cured meat. He showed me a stack of two-inch binders stuffed with legal papers. "It's ridiculous," he said. I asked if he'd ever thought of making his voice heard politically, if he wanted to challenge the system.

"I've never thought about it," he said. All he could do was change the way he ate, perhaps how his community ate.

I looked at the progressive and motivated young people around me, and I felt an aching pit in my stomach as I realized that the bucolic reality they'd created was largely just for themselves. *What about the rest of us?* I thought. Where are the people in our generation who are knocking on doors, demanding subsidies for rotational crops and stricter FDA regulation on antibiotic use? With a mounting farmer deficit, who will address the larger issues—like lack of capital, land access, health care, access to credit and education and training for farmers—that keep many young workers from hopping into agriculture? And then I had the most disheartening thought of all: Do these people exist?

Chapter 7
Pull Up the Weeds

"We're fucked." I looked Jason, my boyfriend of a year, steady in the eyes. "We're fucked," I yelled again, my arms rising in the air.

"Why?" His brow furrowed at my exasperation.

"Because I think this generation actually *is* as narcissistic and self involved as all the critics claim we are." There, I'd said it. After three years of research—interviews, abattoirs, community gardens and food trucks—my secret fear had been confirmed.

I had been hired by *Plate*, a culinary magazine, to write about food policy issues for chefs. I broke down the debates around GMOs, the effects of climate change on our food system, the rapid decline of honeybee populations and the minimum wage. "There are so many problems," I said to Jason. "Big, big, problems. And our generation is doing nothing about it." The latest Farm Bill passed with a cut of $8 billion to food stamps over a decade and expanded crop insurance for agribusinesses that were supplying the corn for Fritos, not the farmer's market.

After returning from Vermont, a few of my habits had changed. At the grocery store, I looked at labels for where my vegetables and fruits were grown. I bought based on seasonality and location at every chance I got. Eventually, I signed up for a CSA—community supported agriculture—in which I paid a membership fee to pick up a bag of fresh fruits and vegetables once a week from a local farm that made drop-offs in Brooklyn. I also started composting, filling a small silver bucket with all my food scraps, and dropping them off each Saturday at the Greenmarket in Prospect Park, and I became more careful about limiting the amount of food I waste each day. But none of it felt significant. It made me feel better about my own contributions as a global citizen, but I didn't feel like I was part of a movement. And we need a movement.

My interest in Generation Yum started at the most surface level: restaurant outings and food media. But eventually I was grabbed by topics far less sexy than finding the airiest beignet in the city. I quickly saw that our food system was the spindle surreptitiously weaving the fabric of American health and environmental wellness, and in its current state, unraveling too much of it. Millennials are going to run this show soon. What are we going to make of it?

I thought back to my journey so far: young people finding connection and stimulation through eating out and cooking, the pleasure of breaking something down to its elements and touching each one, holding the (often literal) fruits of a hard day's work. And while I heard complaints about the larger food system—Giancarlo upset about current laws on livestock treatment, Annie about the inefficiencies of food distribution, and Taylor about Americans' eating habits that neglect "real food"—I didn't feel as though I was any closer to a collective movement. No community was bringing these minds together to solve the many food-related issues we face as a country, and the food movement was still painfully exclusive. Even the radical changes I had seen felt isolated and personal, people fixing what they could right in front of them. And who could really blame them, given the entrenched political and economic systems we've inherited?

But I began to wonder: Are our critics right? Is the Millennial generation, Generation Yum *especially*, just narcissistic and lazy? Will we ever march on the Mall or demand that politicians fix our Farm Bill or fight fracking or advocate in favor of labor rights in numbers resembling the civil rights or women's movements? I flashed back to my trendy but mediocre meal at Bite Club, and my idyllic but isolated experience in Vermont.

While I'd spent a great deal of time attempting to psychologically diagnose Gen Yum, pinpointing the numerous anxiety provoking elements we face and how we react to them, what I'd really found was: We spend a lot of energy on us. Maybe we *are* just self-centered, hopeless, gluttonous kids, using food as a means to cope, not as a way to better the world.

Tim Donovan stands near six feet tall, his bushy, dark beard nearly covering the long dimples around his mouth. Thick-framed square glasses sit across his face, just below the bill of his baseball cap.

On an average afternoon you can find Tim in a garden, either prepping his tomato starts in the tent next to his house, drying tobacco in his yurt, harvesting kale from his urban farm, or directing neighbors in pruning, composting and tilling at the cooperative garden he runs in downtown Portland, Oregon. Tim wears light overalls and thick boots, scuffed from hours upon hours of heavy labor. When he's not in the fields, he's building his new home from local sequoia or training with a knife maker.

When we first chatted in 2012, Tim was the farm director at Project Grow, a nonprofit program of Port City Development Center, where he worked with mentally disabled adults to transform an empty lot into a productive urban garden, selling the produce to local restaurants and members of a CSA program. Rows of lettuce grew in hydroponic greenhouses, chickens clucked around a contained area and Tim instructed participants on how to sow seeds and harvest tomatoes. A year later, Project Grow was in transition and Tim had decided to launch his own project: a cooperative garden and personal garden in two separate Portland locations. He's reaching out to a hospital, nursing home and other nonprofits to bring fresh food to those in need, and farming skills to those who are interested in learning.

"I do this because I love growing food. I always have. It's one of the few things that has consistently kept my attention year after year and my interest in it has only grown," he told me over the phone, during our first conversation. "It's a wonderful process, it's rich, it has amazing natural history, biology, chemistry, geology. It can't ever be boring. I enjoy doing it no matter what." Plus, the deeper purpose, he said, is "totally validating." He sleeps well at night knowing that his actions aren't worsening the environment.

I came to Portland a year later in 2013 hoping to find a subversive subculture, one that was running on its own terms, and I did. My Airbnb host was a raw foodist in the midst of creating a permaculture farm in her backyard (a coincidence on my part). Everything is backwards in Portland. Young people don't work, but they don't seem desperate; frankly, they didn't seem to want to work. Parking lots are filled with food trucks serving gourmet meals at affordable prices. Building supplies are free or close to it: Warehouses sell immense piles of wood and reclaimed home items for pennies. Freeganism—dumpster diving for discarded food from grocery stores and farms with excess or expired products—is commonplace. It seemed like these guys had figured it out: growing their own food, limiting food waste and largely relying on one another, instead of social media, for fulfillment.

While food obsession is perhaps one of the most unique characteristics of the Millennial generation, our failing food system is perhaps the most significant and daunting issue that we do, and will, face. The way Americans grow and consume food is damaging our health, economy and planet. According to the Centers for Disease Control, more than one-third of U.S. adults are obese, including 17 percent of children. Between 1998 and 2006 obesity rates in the United States increased 37 percent, resulting in high rates of cardiovascular disease, type-two diabetes and stroke, even in young children. In 2012, medical costs associated with obesity were estimated at $190 billion, exceeding smoking as public health enemy number one. Obesity-related treatment accounts for 20.6 percent of U.S. healthcare expenditures.

What's more, our eating habits are working against our efforts to fight climate change. The average American eats three times the global norm of meat and poultry, around eight ounces a day. Industrialized livestock production is a worse offender on greenhouse gases than cars. We are seeing massive land erosion, fossil fuel depletion, compromised ecosystems. Forests are being razed so that farmland—and not the idyllic kind I saw in Vermont—can expand to satisfy our ever-increasing demands: more meat, more sugar and more processed foods than ever before. Government subsidies support farmers of corn and soybeans, not organic produce; we have lax regulations on antibiotic use in livestock and abysmal labor laws for seasonal workers. And we dump what we don't eat into costly landfills that contribute even more methane waste into the atmosphere.

"Generation Q," Tom Friedman writes in *The New York Times* op-ed, using his nickname for the Millennials, the "Quiet Americans," "will spend their entire adult lives digging out from the deficits that we—the 'Greediest Generation,' epitomized by George W. Bush—are leaving them," referring to budget, Social Security and ecological deficits.

"America needs a jolt of the idealism, activism and outrage (it must be in there) of Generation Q," he says. "That's what twentysomethings are for—to light a fire under the country. But they can't e-mail it in, and an online petition or a mouse click for carbon neutrality won't cut it. They have to get organized in a way that will force politicians to pay attention rather than just patronize them."

I thought back to my parents. They lived through many revolutionary moments in which young Americans profoundly altered the direction of U.S. policy: civil rights, women's rights. Their generation *made* change by stating their beliefs in the streets, through petitions, votes and pop culture. I wanted to feel, after delving so deeply into my generation's wants, needs and shortcomings, that I could also make a change. But I didn't.

The Millennial Generation now makes up just over a quarter of the United States population. There are more 23-year-olds (4.7 million of them) than any other age group, according to June 2014 census data. Many claim that we have more power than ever: Social media gives us a voice, Kickstarter campaigns give us money and our parents have instilled unreasonable amounts of confidence in us. These ingredients should allow Millennials to change the world, if we really want to. I had assumed that our particular movement—flocking to restaurants, fussing over Instagram images of colorful plates of food and spending our dollars on organic and local goods—would translate into something larger. But if there was a revolution brewing, I hadn't found it yet.

One sunny afternoon, I met up with Tim to learn about urban gardening. Tim is a heady guy. He is dedicated to the details and practicality of farming. Urban gardening, he believes, is important for several reasons. To begin, it's connecting people who might otherwise only see the final product in the supply chain directly with their food source. It's also a productive and low-cost way to utilize vacant land. Finally, it provides genetic diversity in food sources. Project Grow also gives jobs to disabled adults, hand in hand with a feeling of pride and self-sufficiency.

For his own farm, Tim rented an abandoned lot from a friend and turned the soil of the half-acre space, running every bit of dirt through a sieve to extract contaminants and set the foundation for a healthy farm. On one side of the city block plot, a broken down car had rusted into the scenery, blackberry bushes running through it, resting alongside the paneling of a neighboring dilapidated home. On the other end was a smaller, wood house that Tim was building by hand. To the side was a large yurt—Tim's drying house. The farm area itself was pristine: rows of kale, purple broccoli, lettuce. Clover shaded the ground, providing nutrients for the soil.[xviii] As we walked, Tim bent down to break off pieces of the bounty for me to taste: parsley, cilantro, kale flowers.

"Kale flowers. Why the fuck don't people use it? It's way better than broccoli rabe," he exclaimed, shaking his head at the sweet, crisp vegetable diners around the country are missing out on.

He told me about the history of the land, how the Missoula floods scraped away the topsoil and left behind a malnourished slate, and walked me through the methods he uses to feed the soil. When I asked to use the bathroom he shook his head. He didn't have one. Like others I had met in Portland, nearly everything goes right back to the farm. Tim offered me his bucket, to which I replied that I'd wait.

Urbanites across the country, and even overseas, are raising bees and planting herbs on their fire escapes. I even heard of one man keeping rabbits on his roof in Brooklyn. In 2012, William-Sonoma began cashing in on the craze, offering "farm fresh eggs to your table" by selling chicken coops and runs for $879.95. They also offered a shiitake mushroom log, four-tier sprouter kit, DIY cheese kit and a fermentation pot, under the tagline: "homegrown, homemade, home-cooked." "Grow Your Own Food," says a t-shirt sold by community recipe website *Food52*.

In London, there are now nearly 25 honeybee hives for each square mile of the city, as city-dwellers join the "save the bees" movement on their offices or home rooftops. According to a 2014 report by the National Gardening Association, edible gardening in the United States is at its highest levels in a decade. "35% of all households in America," the report states, "or 42 million households, are growing food at home or in a community garden, up 17% in five years." Interestingly (or perhaps not so interestingly at this point) the group participating most is Millennials, up 63 percent, from 8 million to 13 million since 2008. Millennials are also spending boku bucks on food gardening: $1.2 billion in 2013, nearly twice as much as 2008.

These investments are far more time intensive than a dinner out or even an involved meal at home. Farming takes persistent care and attention, developing new habits and maintaining a living thing. Remember, before the baby, before the dog, get a plant.

The media began to focus more intensely on food systems in the mid-2000s. "By 2007 and 2008," write Johnston and Baumann, "we noticed that certain food issues, particularly local eating, sustainability, and animal welfare, were featured in greater depth and with greater frequency. The 'politics of the plate' were in the public eye, well symbolized by the continued media attention and sustained sales of Michael Pollan's tome, *The Omnivore's Dilemma*," which was released in 2006.

In the 2004 documentary *Super Size Me*, Morgan Spurlock ate only McDonald's for a month to shockingly detrimental results. It picked up where bestseller *Fast Food Nation* had left off in 2001. The 2008 film *Food, Inc.* sickened and educated viewers on animal cruelty and the corporate food industry, again with the help of Pollan. This new attention on what *not* to eat, paired with a growing mistrust in the corporate food chain, led many to simply grow their own.

As Tim walked me from his urban garden to another urban oasis, we chatted food trends. While I'd expected him to be thrilled by the vogue excitement in urban farming, he spoke with simmering resentment for Generation Yum. He told me about a recent dinner out with his girlfriend and farmhand, Caroline, at which they witnessed a couple dine without speaking, and intermittently take out their phones to snap pictures of their meal.

"I feel like a lot of people are stuck in the mode of documentation instead of the mode of experience," Tim said, sounding a lot like Greil Marcus. "That ties into my feelings about urban agriculture." The public interest in farming, Tim said, "seems to be done for the fashion of it. A lot of people are doing it to talk about it afterwards; there's this back-patting exercise of like, 'Look what I did.'"

I mentioned my own theories on our generation's need to brand ourselves and receive digital affirmations. Tim, in no uncertain terms, agreed with me, saying that Twitter is a place where people work themselves into a "frenzy" to see if they received the "approval and validation they need." While he appreciates the general public's growing attention on food, his keen eye grasps the selfish motivations apparent in some foodies who post about their farmer-ish projects—like backyard gardens or chicken coops—but then abandon their hens and leave their plants to seed as soon as they're out of fashion. "If gardening is something you really enjoy doing and you're doing it cause you love it, that's all the reason you need," Tim said, resentment filling his sentences, emphasizing the ephemeral interest he observes in others, as he pointed out the lack of genuineness.

His observations harked back to one of my mounting concerns: How honest is this food movement? Thoughts about my generation's self-interest and passivity kept resurfacing—maybe all we really want is a good meal or to pacify our personal anxieties, not to change the world.

For others, their passions for change seem stifled by a 'why bother?' attitude.

"The sense of trust we have in the country, for each other and in major institutions—our journalists, our government—is at the lowest point we've ever measured," said W. Keith Campbell, author of *The Narcissism*

Epidemic: Living in the Age of Entitlement, at a live debate titled: "Millennials Don't Stand a Chance."[xix] (It was a very uplifting evening.) This distrust, of course, is solidly founded. Millennials grew up during the Lewinsky scandal, the political machinations of *Bush v. Gore*, the weapons of mass destruction that never existed. September 11th radically revised our concepts of invincibility and the global economies crashed just as we were about to enter the workforce.

Thomas Friedman asserts that Gen Y is simply too quiet, too subdued, too blasé about important issues. But Millennial Courtney E. Martin challenges this assumption, writing in *The American Prospect*, "I think that [Friedman] has mistaken my generation's sense of being overwhelmed, our absolute paralysis in the face of so many choices, so many causes, and so much awareness, for a mere quiet." The world's woes, she points out, are painfully clear to this generation. We are more connected than any generation prior, bombarded with constant updates, images, videos of atrocities near and far. Just as we find refuge from our technological devices in eating out and cooking, we're overwhelmed as to how we might actually make a difference in the face of the many, many issues that saturate our every moment, both online and off.

"We can't be you, because we don't live in your time," Martin writes, speaking directly to Friedman. "We don't have the benefit of focus, the cushion of cheap rent, the luxury of not knowing just how complicated the world really is. Instead we have corporate conglomerates, private military contracts, the WTO and the IMF, school debt, and no health insurance. We are savvy and we are saturated and we are scared."

"We are not quiet," Courtney Martin writes. "We are often outraged."

Not only are we terrified of the future ahead but we don't trust the government to make the necessary fixes. The general attitude I'd been hearing was: "What's the point of petitioning the government when nothing is going to change? Better to create an oasis for the people I care most about."

"A lot of that activity," Tim said to me, returning to those gardening urbanites, "is fed by these more diluted notions of the positive effect it's actually having. A community garden is not going to confront the great evils of our time, it's not going to take on Monsanto, it's not going to drive gentrification in the neighborhood and create living-wage jobs." He shook his head. I was a bit taken aback. *Did he really just say that?* I thought. *Then why is he doing all this work?*

"People are more afraid, having been burned so many times," Tim explained. "People are not entirely looking toward government or business, they want to hold something in their hands to have some resiliency, agency for survival." Doing something is better than nothing, even if it won't tackle the biggest problems we face. I wondered if Tim was really ok with that. It seemed that he was. He had his farm, and his friends, and he was making the changes within the comfortable boundaries of his world.

"You sure can fix somebody's food–and make a really big difference"

"Young people don't have an outlet for creative revolutionary energies, because you can't do anything about election campaign laws and you can't get the troops out of Afghanistan and Iraq, you can't get corporate America out of Congress. But you sure can fix somebody's food—and make a really big difference. You can do something about your own food, you can do something about your neighbor's food, you can do something about school food, you can do something about institutional food, you can do all that and make a real difference. And you can do it young and see the results, and they're going to be very quick."

I was on a call with Marion Nestle from my Airbnb room in Portland. Nestle, I feel comfortable saying, is the leader of the Food Studies movement. I'd met her (and Bourdain) at a food event. While wandering the room of luminaries, I bumped into Nestle and asked if I could pick her brain, as she spends nearly every day with Millennials hoping to make a change in our food system.

Marion began the Food Studies program at New York University in 1996, along with food consultant Clark Wolf. At the time, cookbook author Paula Wolfert told *The New York Times*: "I don't think a course at N.Y.U. is going to make any difference in regards to public awareness of food's complex contributions to culture, society and personal nutrition." Woops.

Since then, the world of food education has proliferated. You can earn your Ph.D. in Food Studies at Indiana University or major in Sustainable Agriculture and Food Systems at University of California, Davis. The University of Vermont has a Center for Sustainable Agriculture, and the New School, a Food Studies program.

I asked Marion how she interprets the growing interest. "It caught the zeitgeist," she said. "I don't know how else to put it. Or give Michael Pollan credit for it," she said, referring to *The Omnivore's Dilemma*. "I'm happy to do that. I like to think *Food Politics*," Nestle's own book, "had something to do with it. But Michael Pollan certainly had a lot to do with it, because we had people coming in clutching copies of his book and saying, 'This is why I'm here. I wanna study this, I wanna do what he does.' Don't we all?"

Months later I attended the James Beard Foundation Food Conference in New York where I saw Michael Pollan speak on a panel with White House Nutrition Policy Advisor, Sam Kass. The panel was moderated by food writer Jane Black, who posed questions to the outspoken men on what it would take to create a meaningful food movement in Washington. I sat in the audience, cradling my coffee cup and nibbling an apple, thinking about what role Millennials could play in that scenario. As Pollan and Kass left the stage, I jumped at my chance to speak with the author.

Whether Pollan intended to or not, he is responsible for much of the in-depth thinking Millennials now do around the dysfunctional food system. He educated young people about agriculture and somehow made learning about corn genetics and chicken farmers cool. As Nestle said, kids registered for Food Studies programs while holding *The Omnivore's Dilemma* as a touchstone text for life. I had to know what he thought about the members of Gen Yum who have set out to farm, and those of us interested in changing food from our desks. A few weeks after our initial meeting, Mr. Pollan and I found a time to talk over the phone.

"I have a lot of contact with people in this generation," he jumped in on the call, referring to Millennials as well as his time teaching at U.C. Berkeley and speaking at middle schools across the country. "I think that this is a generation that is very politically conscious but is also very interested in hope, and this issue offers hope in a way that very few other issues that we confront do. When you compare the food issue to climate change—of course they're linked in various ways—and the environmental crisis, or the economic crisis, people feel powerless when they confront those huge, intractable problems, and the beauty of the food issue is that, while it is very serious and grave is some ways, there is progress being made."

"My generation had the civil rights movement," Marion Nestle had said to me emphatically, "the anti-Vietnam war movement and the women's movement. We had all that. We were part of social movements that really made a difference. You could measure those differences in the opportunities for women, in the opportunities for minorities." Our generation, she suggested, as well as Pollan did, does not have an issue that we can easily address. What we've turned to instead is our meals.

"I never tire of saying," Pollan remarked on the phone, "that we get three votes a day. We have seen the power of people using their identities as consumers and melding it with their identity as citizens and making choices that are driving a considerable amount of change: the growth of organics, farmers markets and CSAs, and non GMO products. Eating empowers you."

Of course he's right. While the People's Climate March, which brought over 300,000 people to the Big Apple's streets didn't garner nearly as much attention as it should have (try getting anyone's attention in a 24-hour news cycle) we *are* influencing the status quo with our daily shopping habits. Farmer's markets have increased 174 percent since 2000. The U.S. organic market surpassed $31 billion in 2011, up from $1 billion in 1990. Even the Department of Agriculture—generally thought of as the Scrooge of the sustainability movement—started a program called "Know Your Farmer, Know Your Food," to connect consumers with local producers. The desire to know who made our food, where, from what, is growing exponentially. And this is having an enormous, important impact on industry standards and regulation. New York City even implemented a trial municipal compost program in 2014 in hopes of utilizing the city's 100,000 tons of annual food waste to help power the metropolis, following in the footsteps of several West Coast cities.

"There's something fundamentally proto-political about eating," Pollan said. "Your first political decision happens in the high chair when you refuse to eat something. You move your head back and forth and you clench you lips and—even as a little two-year-old—there's nothing adults can do to make you eat. It's the same power that political prisoners use. I think it's very gratifying for people who want to express their political views, who want to embody their values in their lifestyle and don't want to confront the hopelessness of other issues."

Even if some are using food as a fashion statement, they're still participating—going back to the point that Bourdain and Bittman had both made.

"What's different about the food movement today versus in the 60s, and I think it's really different, is that it used to be just a couple of funny people who were off in the woods doing this thing," Nestle said, "and now it's a movement. So in a sense the real difference is quantitative. There are just so many more people involved in this now."

The beauty of it, Pollan ponders, is that food issues can be tackled with or without the government, so our generation's ill toward Congress and political bodies does not entirely hold us back.

"A lot of the food movement is operating outside of the political scale," he explained. "You could conceivably build a new and separate food economy that just kind of rises alongside the big food economy. And we are doing that; it's just still small. But you can't do that with energy, for example."

Today, the processed food sector is readjusting to deal with Millennial preferences a.k.a. declining sales of processed and frozen foods. Meanwhile, Millennials are showing a willingness to pay up for organic goods, more than any other generation.[xx] In 2013, Boston Consulting Group found that Millennial spending will rise for fresh fruits, organic food and natural products, while spending on luxury goods, soda and handbags will decrease.

"Dear Consumers, a disturbing trend has come to our attention. You, the people, are thinking more about health, and you're starting to do something about it. This cannot continue," reads a guest blog post on ScientificAmerican.com, titled "Dear American Consumers: Please Don't Start Eating Healthfully. Sincerely, the Food Industry."

We're already showing signs of major success without taking the traditional routes. We're using Facebook posts and Instagram feeds of our purchases to sway big business, though the poster's intentions may not be as broad as their resulting effects.

Bittman, during our initial conversation, had also claimed that these larger food companies who didn't change their products in the '70s during the macrobiotic movement, or in the early 2000s when Boomers were obsessed with the Atkins diet, are doing it now, "because they have to." The demand is just that large—who cares if people are posting about it on Facebook after? In fact, maybe they should be posting it on Facebook after?

"Food is sexy and hot," Pollan remarked, and "you can be really into foodie culture without having a political bone in your body." He mentioned well-known restaurant reviewers who "really don't give a fuck where their stuff comes from. It's just a pure estheticism."

But, he says, "Maybe you can bring those people along." He gave Mario Batali as an example—a chef with a farm-to-table cookbook who hadn't dipped his toes into political food issues until recently. "It's possible," Pollan said, "that as you develop more of a palate, you develop a curiosity about the system that produces the food that you like or that you find dissatisfying." And in some ways, we're seeing this happen. It's not just a small section of Millennial food policy wonks that is shifting what Big Food serves us—it's the masses.

Perhaps those urbanites who abandon their fire-escape farms are still thinking more about where their food comes from than they were before. Baby steps.

Fast food chains are serving salads and meat free of antibiotics. People are willing to pay six times as much for a burrito at Chipotle than across the street at Taco Bell—only the former has an online TV show about the dangers of industrial farming. These changes may seem minor, but they reflect awareness on the corporate level of the amplifying call for real food. Even McDonald's is trying to reassure a skeptical public that their chicken nuggets do, in fact, contain chicken. Taco Bell's new "high quality" Cantina Bell menu includes ingredients like whole black beans, white-meat chicken, and corn salsa.[xxi] The guacamole, the company says, is made with "100-percent Hass avocado." ("I shudder to think," writes *Boston Globe* staff writer Deborah Katz, "what the traditional Taco Bell guacamole was made from if not 100 percent avocados." As it turns out: sugar, salt, a mix of preservatives such as erythrobic acid and the thickening agent xanthan gum.)

Some believe these small changes propelled by Millennial choices will allay the critical environmental challenges facing the planet. The food movement "may be able to create just the sort of political and social transformation that environmentalists have failed to achieve in recent years," Bryan Walsh wrote in *Time* in 2011. Even if the movement remains isolated to small urban farms, new school lunch programs and a growing interest in organic goods, it could be enough to drive significant environmental improvements. The thought is: If consumers show enough individual interest in organic goods through purchasing powers, conversation, tweeting, whatever, and it's enough to influence a lobbyist or two, perhaps government actions will begin to reflect that demand.

But again, when it comes to the day to day, those I spoke with weren't thinking of their windowsill garden as something revolutionary. They just thought of it as something nice.

"Young people are abandoning the 'save the world' rhetoric we were raised with," Courtney E. Martin writes, "and seeking out a more practical, complex analysis of social change. We don't want to 'save the world.' We're too smart to think we can.[xxii] We want to live in it—flawed, fierce, loving, and humble."

"Small is beautiful again," she continues. "We're still committed to making broken systems (education, healthcare, prison etc.) more just, but if today, right now, all we can do is make one person's day within that system more kind, fair, or dignified, we'll devote ourselves wholeheartedly to it."

In Martin's writing, I see Tim and Annie and Taylor and all the other innovators I had met who were determined to change what they could, and not fret over what they couldn't. There still is not a clear path to making major change within food policy. All you can do is hope that your small contributions will lend themselves to a bigger wave.

"Bad news, kids," begins a comic written by Millennial Zachary Weiner. An older bearded gentleman with thick-framed glasses, drawn with a shiny, bare, crowned head stands before two young adults. "I've decided to ignore economic data and assume the challenges facing your generation are the same as those mine faced."

"Oh no!" the terrified young'uns reply, looking up at their elder.

"Worse," the man states, "I'm going to assume you want what I wanted! And when you fail to strive for it, I will perceive that as laziness."

"Nooo!" the aghast kids reply. "How can we help?" they ask.

"When I was your age," the older man says, "we *knew* how to help."

Disruption

Back in New York, I was still battling conflicting feelings. Will these small movements continue to lead to wider change? I'd love to believe in Bryan Walsh's theories, but I wasn't sold. An urban garden, after all, is nothing revolutionary. And McDonald's and Taco Bell could easily revert to their cost-cutting, processed ways if the tide turned once again. It's fine to fix what you can in front of you, but will that ultimately create a new food distribution system, adequately address global warming and hunger in

America? It was still difficult to find farm-fresh produce in the Brooklyn supermarkets in late 2013, early 2014. I was fortunate enough to live near a weekend farmer's market and co-op, but much of the rest of the borough wasn't so lucky.

"Why don't you try Good Eggs?" a friend asked me one afternoon over lunch. I'd never heard of it. "They deliver food from farms," he said. "It's like Fresh Direct but from farmers instead of grocery stores."

My mouth dropped. Genius! Why hadn't it been done before? Screw the grocery store, pick up directly from the producer. While it's easier for those living close to farmland, the option for urbanites had never existed. Until now.

I went home and logged onto their website. I could see what their farmers would be harvesting that week and choose from multiple purveyors. And who did I see right away? Annie Myers, now with her own farm in Vermont, Myers Produce. I could eat Annie's veggies, in Brooklyn. Huzzah!

Good Eggs had been online for about a year, first in San Francisco. Slowly, it had migrated east. Other similar concepts quickly popped up: Farmigo, Farmbox Direct, Relay Foods and Greenling, all offering organic, farm goods, delivered to your home. While some charged hefty fees—think the Whole Foods of farm delivery—other programs, like Fresh FoodBox, were primarily focused on underserved communities. "A $10 FoodBox is filled with $9.50 worth of produce from New York farms, which would retail at a grocery store at about $26," the *New York Observer* reported. The rest of the costs are covered by donations and grants.

For those who don't even want to make the trip to the store for the necessary items (oil, vinegar, butter, etc.) to make a meal, other startups are encouraging would-be restaurant goers to cook at home with hand-holding services like Blue Apron and Plated, which deliver portioned ingredients and brightly-printed instructions.

In the summer of 2014, I was invited to a food and technology hackers event hosted by Food + Tech Connect, a small company focused on food technology and innovation. Nearly 200 designers and developers joined forces to brainstorm technological solutions for food system challenges set forth by Applegate, Chipotle Mexican Grill, Batali & Bastianich Hospitality Group, Google and Studio Industries.

"We're here to create real world solutions for real world problems," Food + Tech Connect's CEO and co-founder (and Millennial) Danielle

Gould said. Teams paired up and pitched their concepts to a panel of experts, including chef Wylie Dufresne and Naveen Selvadurai of Foursquare. The event was held at General Assembly, a startup that focuses on affordable classes to give Gen Yers practical skills, like coding and inDesign. The open space was buzzing with excitement, attendees gathered around tables of cheese and crackers, Chipotle burritos and buckets of Brooklyn Brewery beers. The initial pairing off of teams occurred the day before, and the hackers had spent the last 24 hours hashing out their ideas, creating wireframes and planning their presentations. No one in the room, besides the judges and company reps, was over 30.

The presentations were a mixed bag, some with creative solutions, and others that left the judges dazed and confused. One team, while attempting to answer the question put forth by Chipotle, "How might we use technology to help quick service restaurants (QSR) measure the environmental sustainability of how their stores are designed, built, and operated?" suggested a complex system in which customers could order by app while waiting in line, allowing them to choose precise measurements of each ingredient for their burritos, in order to minimize food waste. One of the judges, Richard Corraine, COO of Union Square Hospitality Group, looked on with a stupefied stare. "Why not just make small, medium, and large options?"

While some of the ideas were not revolutionary, many were exciting. There were so many young creatives clamoring to participate that organizers had to turn people away. Perhaps, I began to think, the most provocative subversions of the food movement will happen where much Millennial-driven change begins: in technology and new business initiatives.

"In a world buffeted by change, faced daily with new threats to survival, the only way to conserve is by innovating," writes management expert Peter Drucker. Millennials are better innovators, or at least faster innovators, than any generation before. While the government and other institutions have stalled on making important changes, we've pushed ahead. For better or worse, we've altered the book industry with blogging, television with YouTube, the music business with Spotify, and hospitality services with Uber, Lyft and Airbnb.

"If we took the approach of, 'Hey, let's wait and see what the government does to create a path that is very, very clear'… we wouldn't be operating anywhere," John Zimmer, the cofounder and president at Lyft, a ride-share program, said during a Freakonomics podcast in 2014. Instead, Lyft has entirely altered public transportation in San Francisco without government approval, and received $700 million in investments in April, 2014.

"Over the past generation," wrote David Bornstein, author of *How to Change the World*, in *The New York Times*, "the world has seen a marked increase in the number of people who have the capacity to be change-makers. At the same time, because of the pace of change and the information revolution, more people are aware that institutions—especially governments and businesses—are failing to address big problems in the environment, the economy and education."

In July 2014 alone, venture capitalists invested nearly $740 million in the food technology and media sector. In September 2014, Good Eggs raised $21 million to expand their delivery program to other cities. Technologies are revolutionizing how farmers test their soil for nutrients and track rainfall; transforming landfill waste into a source of energy; tracking calorie intake for SNAP program participants; and turning the concept of "home gardening" on its head with indoor hydroponic farms. "Food Startups Are Riding A VC Gravy Train," announced *TechCrunch*. Millennials are grabbing the bull by the horns to disrupt any aspect of food distribution, energy and hunger that they can, all through technology, all on their own.

Ripe For the Taking

"I often ask audiences," Michael Pollan told me: "'How would you feel if McDonald's went all organic, grass-fed, or Coca-Cola went organic?' And the audience always boos. They're disappointed; they don't want this to happen. It's not their idea of a happy future. Even though from a substantive point of view that would represent a tremendous victory, quite a victory for the environment—all that land that wouldn't be treated with atrazene and other terrible chemicals. But people really want more than that. They want a new food economy. They don't just want to fix the old one."

I was feeling inspired by my latest conversations: Pollan pointing out all that *has* been achieved through small pro-food actions (be it social media posts, farm-to-table dinners or a bevy of homemade pickle shops opening their doors), and all the latest investment heading into food and technology startups. I could see the percolation of change. But to Pollan's point, we don't just want a bigger organic aisle or gluten-free taquitos from Taco Bell. We want a new food economy. Not to be too obvious, but that is a big task, and it's not going to come to fruition without massive and collective social and economic shifts, and I'm not sure tweeting or apps are going to get us there.

"The challenge with the food movement, if you compare it to gay rights or the Civil Rights Movement, is that there are too many different issues in the Food Movement," Michael Pollan analyzed. Food, he argues, relates to so many different facets of life that it's hard to create a cohesive campaign for change. "People are in [the Food Movement] because they care about animals; people are in it because they care about climate change; people are in it because they care about public health, and even though sustainable agriculture kind of supports all those goals, people are not all on the same page."

"One of the things that the Food Movement needs to do," he outlined, "is settle on a list of priorities or a first priority in the same way that gay marriage became the issue of the Gay Rights Movement. Everyone coalesced around gay marriage. That wasn't a given," he noted. "That had to be decided on and forced by certain participants."

"The Food Movement is somewhat hindered by its lack of organization and lack of leadership. I mean, it's lead by a bunch of writers and chefs," he quipped. "That's not the recipe for successful politics. But that will change and that's what I look to in your generation," he said to me. "You have people who went to law school because they were convinced that was the path to change the food system. You have people who went to public policy school, who went to food studies programs who are developing a kind of toolkit for leadership that the movement sorely needs. I'm kind of counting on this generation to pull things together."

Food "is an issue of engaging the senses," Pollan said to me, echoing my own beliefs. "It's not purely abstract; it's something that you can enact and feel and taste and I don't know why that's particularly of interest to this generation, but I think it is. I think getting your hands dirty is very important. It's a sign of authenticity and commitment, that you're not just talking about it, you're doing it, and food lends itself to that in a way that very few other issues do."

"The fact that [Millennials] spend so much time in front of a screen makes cooking and eating and growing food all the more attractive," he went on. This, he believes, along with the fact that "you can make your politics and your lifestyle and your professional life all one through farming or working in food systems," sets up Generation Yum as the future leaders for food policy change.

The idea is: If we, Yummers, can agree on one issue to push forward, we can generate collective momentum. Then, all the Millennials who are getting their degrees in food studies and food policy and creating stellar apps can take that momentum and run with it to create even more substantial change.

Of course, I like this idea. I love the notion that we will be the ones who lead the Food Movement to joyous success. But a few things still hold me back from jumping into the "Yay, we can save the world!" pool.

My biggest concern about the legacy of Generation Yum still hinges on our central characteristic: self-interest. Food has become a movement because it serves *us* well. We create community, experience sensory pleasure, feelings of accomplishment and personal satisfaction through what we farm, cook and eat. Organics and GMOs are easy to address on the individual scale, and they became fetishized in the marketplace. Organic produce is deemed superior. The anti-GMO craze piggybacked on the larger trend of demanding to know what is in our food. Not all topics are this accessible.

If improvements to U.S. food policy are going to continue to take place based on public demands, the next issue we prioritize has to be something that plays into the needs and wants of Millennials. It has to be actionable, each and every day. It needs to be tangible, a choice people can hold and see. It needs to be something that can potentially be fetishized, a choice that can be touted as 'so cool' or 'super awesome.' As many have said, change looks different today, but that doesn't mean it doesn't or can't exist.

Millennials' apparent detachment from an analog "reality" and connection to technology makes us crave tangible, immediately perceptive change. We enjoy what we can participate in. We want to help a community garden take root, teach a food education class or develop an app for our friends to download and interact through, pairing them with restaurants that source sustainable produce or share vegan recipes. Yet we still need to tackle the larger issues: fracking, food waste, farmer rights and subsidies, soda bans, fish fraud and so many others. We need to change big picture food policy, and unfortunately, there is no app for that.

Chapter 8
The Final Ingredient

As I near the end of my Gen Yum journey—at least, in book form—I've been forced to ask myself some tough questions. "I'm kind of counting on this generation to pull things together," Pollan said to me. After years of poking holes in my own obsession and habits, and delving deeper into the mess of a food system we have, I still think back to the cartoon where the old man screeches: "When I was your age, we *knew* how to help."

While at times my thoughts are awash in negative hopelessness for our generation, there are clear signs that this may be too fatalistic of me. Yes, Yummers most often engage with food for selfish reasons: decadent tastes, guest compliments, adventures we can brag about. But there is one thing that reminds me that the future is bright for Gen Yum: We *love* food. We appreciate the farmers and their artistry—a perfectly seared salmon steak or a salted turnip harvested with the utmost care. We like eating together and leaving the city to go apple picking. Though we could stay plugged in 24/7, it's not what we're choosing to do.

We've proven with the organics movement and non-GMO labeling that us Yummers *can* create bigger change, it just doesn't look like the movements of yesteryear.

I thought quite a bit about Pollan's assignment: decide on a priority for the Food Movement. And maybe I took him too literally, or too personally, but I decided on something— something that I think Yummers and Xers and Boomers and you can act on to make change.

One of the most easily accessible, understandable and actionable items on that ever-growing list of food issues—and the area where I can see Yummers making waves next—is food waste. Food waste is any food that's disposed of, such as leftovers, ugly fruits and vegetables that farmers can't sell to grocery chains, or items that expire or spoil. In the U.S., 40 percent of all food is wasted. In money terms, that's $165 billion worth of food annually. In daily life context, that's nearly every other piece of food you purchase going un-consumed, or $28 to $40 bucks per person squandered each month. For your bank account, subtract $336 to $480 each year.

Food waste causes a number of problems. Firstly, organic waste breaks down. During that process of decomposition, waste creates methane, which contributes to greenhouses gasses and climate change. Some areas around the world are smartly beginning to harness that methane for energy. But when the waste goes into a garbage can instead of an anaerobic digester, you can be certain that that half-eaten salad or extra taco is not going lend itself to anything productive (and food disposal, by the way, costs the U.S. another $750 million per year).

Along with that tossed out taco is the labor, water, pesticides, and all the nutrients that were used to make the lettuce, tomato, avocado, masa harina, pork or any other ingredient. In terms of wasted water, throwing out half a hamburger is equivalent to taking over an hour shower, according to the Water Footprint Network. 25 percent of all freshwater, along with four percent of oil, is entirely wasted on making food products.

On top of that, one in six Americans is food insecure, meaning they don't know where their next meal is coming from. If we all started to utilize food more thoughtfully, therefore wasting less and purchasing less, there would be more resources for those who go hungry. It's even possible that prices would drop to entice consumers to buy more, opening the market up to those who currently can't afford pricy organic goods. If we ate the "ugly" foods from farmers, farmers would make more money. They could then invest more in their farmland and produce even more consumable food. Wasting less food would influence water conservation, greenhouse gas emissions, hunger, municipal waste programs, and oil demand.

So how do you waste less food? About two-thirds of household waste is due to food not being eaten in time, whereas the other third is caused by cooking and buying too much. There are some simple ways to avoid this.

Take on the #WasteLessChallenge (a challenge that I am devising right here, right now) to only throw out 10 liters of trash a week (that's the size of a small trash can, or what will fill one generic plastic bag). While this may seem crazy at first, it's totally possible to do, likely without changing much of what you consume, just how you dispose of what you don't.

So what are the best ways to reduce your waste?

Compost. Buy yourself a shiny or colorful compost bin that you don't mind having around. Add any plant waste to the bin. Either drop it off at a local garden or farmer's market, or compost it yourself in the backyard. Get a bin with a carbon filter to avoid any nasty smells. I highly recommend adding leaves or newspaper to keep it from getting too runny. It's a pretty amazing process to watch all your food scraps turn into dark, nutrient rich soil.

Locally, demand municipal compost—to be used to build local gardens and parks—and anaerobic digesters, which process the methane released from waste to create energy. That would mean less greenhouse gas emissions and lower energy bills. Also, call on your local government to regulate waste. In Seattle, those with over 10 percent recyclables or food waste in their garbage are fined.

Recycle. These days, almost all packaging is reusable. Got a to-go cup of coffee? Add the top to the plastic pile and the cup to the paper pile. Better yet, carry around a reusable mug. Whenever possible, avoid buying products in Styrofoam. In fact, when you can, avoid food in packaging. All that plastic uses up tons of resources—gas, oil, water and chemicals. Leave the extras behind—all you need is real food.

Eat what you buy. Americans are accustomed to super-sized meals, but we can't stomach all that's put on the oversized plates. The average person wastes 240 pounds of food a year. Pay attention to how much you actually eat and only purchase foods that you know you'll finish. Whatever you can't get to, freeze it or compost it.

Upcycle. Become an advocate for leftovers. There are so many ways to give a face-lift to half-eaten grub. Save certain kitchen scraps for stock; I always have a plastic bag with onion and garlic peels, the fronds of fennel and unused carrot tops collecting in my freezer. Un-eaten vegetables can be pickled, fruits frozen for smoothies or simmered into jam.

Talk to your local grocer and ask them to start a program for imperfect and expired foods. Supermarkets play a big role in food waste. The USDA estimates that supermarkets toss out $15 billion worth of unsold fruits and vegetables each year. That's not including the cans of Campbell's French Onion soup that end up in the dumpster as they pass their "consume by" date, or the fruits and vegetables left to fester in farm fields because they don't fit grocers' beauty standards.

Cook with the underdogs. Choose the rotational crops, less popular grains and cuts of meat. Keep in mind—a whole lamb was raised to get those lamb chops. What happens to the rest of it? With Dan Barber in mind, eat the third plate—items that are perhaps not in fashion culinarily, but certainly tasty and important for the continued health of our agriculture. This step helps reduce waste in the larger food system.

By taking action against food waste, Yummers can become change-makers in a hugely impactful way. Think about all we've done already in terms of organic and non-GMO foods and school lunches. Maybe we haven't made food a top voter's issue yet, but Yummers are certainly causing change through purchasing powers and vocalizing our opinions on social media.

What if the #WasteLessChallenge became a trend? Can you imagine if all food and recyclables were no longer going to landfills? If there was a table of cheaper imperfect produce at the supermarket? If local gardens and parks popped up, made with waste-transformed soil? If local governments saved money by driving less trucks to dump waste, and used methane to fuel city buildings? If farmers could make more money by selling *all* their crops, even the ones that wouldn't be donned pageant queen? If restaurants could offer cheaper meals by spending less money on excess ingredients and reusing scraps? If population growth wasn't inevitably tied to more hungry people? If the largest food corporations and supermarkets bettered their packaging and disposal practices? If there were 1,000 recipes for broccoli and cauliflower stems on Pinterest? You can help make that change.

Just as Pollan says, you get three votes a day. But you actually get to vote again as you decide how to dispose of what you haven't consumed. So make that six votes a day. Vote with every food choice you make, and again when you choose how to dispose of what's leftover.

Most recently, the topic of food waste has been buzzing across social media feeds as foodie icons make upcycled meals Instagram ready. At the forefront are chefs Dan Barber and Roy Choi, who in 2015 launched independent restaurant projects that aim to re-use food waste. For three weeks in March of 2015, Dan Barber opened wastED, a pop-up housed in his famous Manhattan restaurant, Blue Hill. The menu incorporated a variety of food scraps: skate wings, mango skins, beef tallow, kale ribs, ugly vegetables and more.

"If there's an endgame, it's how does this stuff get bumped up?" Barber told *The New Yorker*'s Hannah Goldfield. "Lobster, maybe seventy years ago, was fed to prisoners. Actually, there was a law that said you couldn't feed lobster meat more than once a week to prisoners, because it was inhumane." Maybe vegetable pulp burgers or caramelized pineapple cores are the lobster of tomorrow.

Later in 2015, West Coast chefs Roy Choi and Daniel Patterson plan to open Loco'l, a waste(less) fast food chain that will repurpose food scraps, utilize bulk orders of ingredients and incorporate sustainable preparation practices. The business model is based on the frugal savings generated by simply throwing out less. This, in turn, will allow them to offer cheaper menu items. "We're aiming to revolutionize the fast food industry as we know it in America," Choi and Patterson write on their Indiegogo crowdfunding site. "It's going to be [a] long, difficult and damn near impossible journey." Instead of fortifying a burger with pink slime or other chemical compounds, Choi and Patterson are going Mom-style: using up leftovers.

The trend can sponge off of the Yummer DIY obsession: turning wood shipping pallets into raised beds, beer bottles into chandeliers and gas pipes into shelving units. Finally chefs are showing the general public that you don't have to be a hippie to think that onion peels, mushroom stumps and pig ears are worth saving and using.

The End?

In September of 2014, Jason and I got engaged.

"Where do you want to get married?" I asked him.

"A barn," he replied. "In the fall."

I nodded. I could do a barn. I could see the rustic, worn-down wood panels with light peeking in, decorations of seasonal fruits and vegetables along with wildflowers, rose-gold votive candles and farm-to-table, family-style dishes. I loved the idea of finding a place a bit off the beaten path, a place far away from our day-to-day lives of New York City subways, muted office spaces and iced lattés. Though I hadn't moved to a farm, I really loved the idea of getting married on one. I knew my parents would think we were nuts.

"Apparently this is a thing," my father later commented, shrugging at our not-so-out-of-the-box plans. He was hearing that many people my age were traveling outside their urban centers to marry on sunlit, grassy farmland. It didn't make much sense to him, but if it made me happy, he was fine with it.

Many use weddings as a time to make a most opulent dream a reality. Couples marry in ornate mansions, hotels or historic buildings; they fly to the shores of Hawaii or Italy to say their vows with the waves of the Pacific ocean or Amalfi coast whispering behind them; they wear ball gowns and jewels fit for royalty.

But we really preferred the plot of vegetable-sown land surrounded by apple orchards and waving stalks of corn on the family-owned, organic Illinois farm. There is a small farmhouse where we can get ready with family, a huge tree to hold the ceremony under, a donkey and two baby goats who hang out in the pen right next to the event area, a bee farm and organic veggies sprouting in rows.

I am a Yummer, through and through. I cook to entertain, to soothe, to project a brand. I find immense pleasure in dissecting recipes, learning how to make whiskey and plant an urban garden. And while I know that the farm wedding may be hipster chic—Mason jars, mismatched China and burlap runners—I can't imagine a more bucolic or romantic place to be married. It's everything I crave, in one magical space.

With the years of research put into this generation, I've realized that, yes, Millennials are narcissistic. We *are* self-involved. We have to be. We were told that if we just followed the path laid out for us—from debate team to SAT prep to college to a stable, linear career—everything would turn out at least as well as it did for our parents. But unemployment rates for 2008 college graduates remain higher than for graduates overall, and our salaries have yet to catch up to peers just a few years ahead of us. We're reminded constantly that maintaining several varieties of digital "brand" is necessary for advancement in both work and play (how else will you get a job or a date?). We've been disillusioned by endemic corporate greed and looming environmental disasters and a deadlocked political system. We've had to pave our own way.

We're not marching in the streets or knocking on doors. We're tweeting, hashtagging and cooking. We make political issues yet another form of social currency. We are shifting our buying habits. We are incessantly talking about food.

I await the day when others will scorn if they see someone toss a plastic container in the trash, if lights are left on all day or if compost bins are not readily available. Just how sea urchin udon is sexy, I want hydroponic, home grown bows of purple basil, CSA bounties of watermelon radishes and mycelium to-go containers to be oh so "on fleek." My goal is to have all the Yummers who think about recipes and restaurants to also care about where those ingredients come from and what those foods are packaged in, how they're transported and how those who grow that food are being compensated and supported through the government.

But as Pollan notes, we have to start one issue at a time to generate the collective energies for larger change, and I hope that food waste is the next issue that Yummers view as hip and sexy and impactful.

Soon, I'll be walking down the aisle flanked by rows of kale, and red and yellow apple trees. Going forward, I'll continue to push myself to see how I can contribute, as a Yummer, to the Food Movement.

As us Yummers we grow up, I hope that we'll take these lessons and our passion for food, and pass it on. The trends discussed in this book—all the details about why this new generation of adults is so fervently attached to food—will only be more relevant in the years to come. Millennials will be the policy makers and our children's lives will be even more saturated with clicks, beeps, and buzzes. This means that the need for connection, control, tangibility and sensory exploration will only become more drastic over time.

I hope we feed our kids, not just with awesome, organic goods, but with an agricultural education that reminds them that though Power Point presentations may crash, and stock markets are unpredictable, and no, we have no idea how to help them with their coding homework, they can go outside, stick their hands in the ground, gently fold in a seed and watch it grow. They can care for it with all the things nature provides: sunlight, water and warmth. I hope we remind them that nothing is a substitute for in-person relationships, that how they live affects the planet and that there is no better way to connect with others than by sharing a meal.

Epilogue
How to Take Action

Here is a list of more easy steps you can take each and every day to live a bit more sustainably.

1. Eat Less Meat.

• If everyone in the U.S. reduces their meat consumption by 20 percent, it will have the same environmental impact as all drivers switching to hybrid vehicles. I'm not saying, "eat vegetarian" or "eat vegan" just eat *less* meat. Consider it a treat, a garnish, a side. Not the main course.

2. Buy local.

• This applies to everything really, from pizzas to furniture. Buy from local makers, local purveyors, local farmers. Whatever the shortest distance is that a good has to travel, the greener it is. Plus, buying locally also often means you're supporting small businesses or farmers and probably means you're buying real food. Bonus!

3. Reuse Water.

• You don't have to skip showers to save some H_2O. Got some stinky water from a vase? Pour it on your outdoor plants instead of down the drain.

4. Turn off the lights.

• You've been hearing it since you were a kid: Turn off the lights when you leave the room. It's still good advice.

5. Use Social Media

• If you're making your life a little more green: Show it off. Get others involved. If you have a trick for making stock out of food scraps, Facebook it. Plant some awesome herbs at home? Pin it. Find a stellar butcher that sources responsibly? Yelp it!

6. Vote.

- You probably know Tom Colicchio for his *Top Chef* evaluations or Craft restaurants, but he's also behind a website that makes it super easy for you to know how your local politicians have voted on food policy issues. Check out Food Policy Action to learn more about your representatives, and make it known that your vote relies on them helping us build a safe food system.

For more tips on how to live sustainably, check out my blog, Generation Yum, at www.eveturow.com/genyum. And if you take on the #WasteLessChallenge let me know @EveTurow.

Acknowledgments

I'd like to take a few sentences to give my utmost thanks to everyone and anyone who helped me write this book. My research into Generation Yum was not intended to be a book-length work, but the engaging interviews, persistent insights and new avenues continued to present themselves and I decided to keep walking that path. Thank you to my professors at the The New School who helped me craft the beginning stages of this book. Thank you to Nina Shield for editing these sentences time and again, to my parents for reading copious drafts, to my agent, Angela Miller, for believing in this project, and to my friends and family for never telling me to stop talking about food. Thank you to those who let me into their homes, on their farms and into their restaurants as I peppered them with questions. I am immensely grateful to all the incredible writers, researchers and chefs who gave me their time, their thoughts and their attention. To Mark Bittman for throwing me into the gauntlet of food media, and my editors since then for continuing to make me a better writer. Thank you, above all, to Jason, for your continued to support as I've battled the endless writing, editing and publishing process. I look forward to a lifetime of delicious meals together.

---

[i] A spokeswoman for Paul Hobbs Winery in California says Millennials are "arguably going to be the largest, most influential customer group the wine market has ever seen."

[ii] According to a report by the Economic Policy Institute, young college graduates, those aged 21 to 24 years old, are facing record high unemployment and underemployment rates. In 2011, 9.4 percent were unemployed and 19.1 percent underemployed. The Bureau of Labor

[ii] According to a report by the Economic Policy Institute, young college graduates, those aged 21 to 24 years old, are facing record high unemployment and underemployment rates. In 2011, 9.4 percent were unemployed and 19.1 percent underemployed. The Bureau of Labor Statistics' (BLS) U-6 Alternative Measure of Labor Underutilization—defines underemployment as: "Unemployed, plus all persons marginally attached to the labor force, plus total employed part time for economic reasons, as a percent of the civilian labor force plus all persons marginally attached to the labor force." In laymen's terms, anyone who is working part time who wants to be working full time, plus the unemployed, who are those currently looking for work.

[iii] And while Millennials are the most educated generation it doesn't seem to be doing much good. Nearly one in three graduates fill jobs they could have obtained without a degree. "The U.S. now has 115,000 janitors with college degrees, along with 83,000 bartenders, 80,000 heavy-duty truck drivers, and 323,000 waiters and waitresses," writes John Leo in "Janitors With College Degrees and the Higher-Education Bubble" on *The Daily Beast*.

[iv] The "sharing economy" phenomenon has rocked the industrial to the point that businesses are reworking their tactics. In 2013, lawyer Janelle Orsi published *Practicing Law in the Sharing Economy: Helping People Build Cooperatives, Social Enterprise, and Local Sustainable Economies*, to

outline the legal matters surrounding collaborative consumption. In 2010, Rachel Botsman and Roo Roger focused on peer economies in their book *What's Mine Is Yours: The Rise of Collaborative Consumption.*

v According to the *Washington Examiner.* "Conventional group membership, attendance at meetings, working with neighbors, trusting other people, reading the news, union membership and religious participation are all down for young people since the 1970s."

vi Case defines cyborgs as an organism "to which exogenous components have been added for the purpose of adapting to new environments."

vii California has crafted what some are calling an "eraser law" that gives under 16 Internet users the ability to delete any information online that they have previously posted. In essence, it protects their digital skeletons from a lifetime of sharing. Posted nude photos of yourself at 15 and now you're concerned about college? California believes you have the right to take that down.

viii Millennial disinterest in driving is a major concern for car companies who readily admit the shifting trend is pushing down sales. "The car used to be the signal of adulthood, of freedom," Sheryl Connelly, the Ford Motor Company's manager of global consumer trends told *The New York Times.* "It was the signal into being a grown-up. Now, the signal into adulthood for teenagers is the smartphone." Now, kids don't want to drive because it interrupts texting time. Freedom is not found on the road, but in their digital profiles.

ix For those confused by this example, "Dude Where's My Car?" is a teen-focused motion picture released in 2000 in which two stoners wake up from a festive evening and can't remember where they parked their car. Yes, that is the entire basis of the movie.

x In the land of fun facts, in a study by BBDO, 88 percent of Millennials admitted they check their phones at the dinner table, but 44 percent said they hate it when others do it. (We're so reasonable.)

xi A survey published in the American Sociological Review shows that the average number of personal confidants has decreased from 2.94 people in 1985 to 2.08 in 2004, essentially one fewer person. Additionally, "the modal number," the number that appears most often, "of discussion partners has gone from three to zero, with almost half of the population (43.6 percent) now reporting that they discuss important matters with either no one or with only one other person." What's the point of bringing up these numbers? They perfectly showcase the Internet's insufficiencies in allowing us to discuss important matters. Instead of discussing important matters with more people, which one might expect as we're more "connected" than ever, people aren't discussing important issues with nearly anyone. Instead of producing meaningful relationships, the Internet simply demands our attention for several hours, yet in the end, leaves us lonely.

xii As of November, 2014, chef Anthony Bourdain boasts 1.91M followers, chef Gordon Ramsay has 1.97M, and chef Jamie Oliver has a whopping 4.07M

xiii Something to keep in mind: more people are using Pinterest today than Twitter.

xiv College kids have even invented a new form of peer pressure: The Instagram Diet. College students are posting their meals online for others to peruse and, well, judge. It means not eating anything that will embarrass you if others can see it. Thus, no fried, fatty foods. Diet bars and vegetables are fair play. It's peer pressure when your peers aren't around.

xv If devouring a Chicken McNugget, your body is about to process a whole lot more than chicken. Traditional Chicken McNuggets are filled with modified food starch, salt, seasoning, which is comprised of autolyzed yeast extract, salt, wheat starch, natural flavoring (botanical source), safflower oil, dextrose, and citric acid, sodium phosphates, and natural flavor (botanical source). The only thing I recognize on that list is salt. And that's just what's on the inside. Plus, who knows what parts of the chicken are actually being used, and what those chickens have been treated with or fed.

xvi To better educate shoppers at the grocery store, Animal Welfare Approved (AWA), a standard third party certification, created a document titled "Food Labeling for Dummies." In the introduction of the packet the company outlines many of the misleading icons, statements and claims made on food. "Let's consider a package of meat labeled 'All natural Angus beef,'" they write. "Looking at this label, you might assume that this cow has spent every day of her life on lush grass in beautiful countryside. But the reality is that from six months of age it lived on a feedlot, where it was routinely treated with antibiotics. It never saw another blade of grass for the remainder of its life and was fed a grain-based diet in a feedlot until the day it was slaughtered. To top it all, the cow actually had no real Angus heritage in the first place – she simply had a predominantly black hide, which is all that was needed to qualify the farmer to use this term. In fact, the only true word in the 'All natural Angus beef' label is that it was beef. This kind of misleading labeling is not only legal, but widely used." Examples such as this mystify purchases and are indeed a key catalyst for increased food labeling and less opaque food processing.

xviiIn the US today, for each farmer under 35, there are six over 65. The National Young Farmers' Coalition hopes to inspire more young people to farm, in order to secure America's farming future.

xviii "Little bacterium that sit on the fruits, the little pink nodules, nitrobacter rhizobium, those take the atmospheric nitrogen and turn it into useable nitrates for the plant—takes it out of the air, puts it into the soil," Tim explained. "It does good work for us. We're always trying to compare different kinds of clover."

xix A survey by Pew found that just 19% of Millennials say most people can be trusted, compared with 31% of Gen Xers, 37% of Silents and 40% of Boomers.

xx 58% of Millennials will pay more for organic and natural, versus 43% for Baby Boomers.

xxiMcDonald's launched an on-point commercial in 2015 that claims, "the days when things were simpler are back" with their Artisan Grilled Chicken. Another version of the same commercial gives a nod directly to Gen Y, claiming that they're not trying to pull a prank—the commercial has "no dancing millennials." The chicken is for real…maybe.

xxii "Tom Brokaw, champion of the Greatest Generation, loves millennials," writes Joel Stein in *Time Magazine*. "He calls them the Wary Generation, and he thinks their cautiousness in life decisions is a smart response to their world. 'Their great mantra has been: Challenge convention. Find new and better ways of doing things. And so that ethos transcends the wonky people who are inventing new apps and embraces the whole economy.'"